Beyond Artificial Intelligence

Series Editor
Abdelkhalak El Hami

Beyond Artificial Intelligence

*From Human Consciousness to
Artificial Consciousness*

Alain Cardon

WILEY

First published 2018 in Great Britain and the United States by ISTE Ltd and John Wiley & Sons, Inc.

ISTE Ltd
27–37 St George's Road
London SW19 4EU
UK

www.iste.co.uk

John Wiley & Sons, Inc.
111 River Street
Hoboken, NJ 07030
USA

www.wiley.com

Library of Congress Control Number: 2018947906

British Library Cataloguing-in-Publication Data
A CIP record for this book is available from the British Library
ISBN 978-1-78630-359-2

Contents

Table of Definitions

Chapter 2. The Computer Representation of an Artificial Consciousness

Introduction

Artificial intelligence is concerned with the development of computer systems that simulate human reasoning when they are applied to the domain of rational knowledge. More specific subdomains are structured by ontologies, which enable the development of systems that use this knowledge with great subtlety when questions are posed to them. This is true today of all computers and small portable devices that enable communication via the Internet on countless websites. All of these systems are therefore made to replace specialists and to help humans with their endeavors. Evolution has led to a connection between computer science and the physical, especially the electronic, which has made it possible to introduce rational behaviors into physical systems whose behavior is thereby rendered autonomous. This is how robotization has developed and continues to progress. The human being considers themselves as the pre-eminent creator, supervisor and decision-making user of these systems. This is no longer the case, since the user of a tablet or smart phone is not on their tablet or smart phone but in the device's native environment. These devices can communicate autonomously via a Hertzian network with remote systems and can make recommendations that were absolutely not requested, all while refining the user's consumer profile.

And they can do much more. These computerized systems, all of which are systems with processors and memory, can be equipped with the ability to generate forms of intentional thoughts, to have desires and needs, and to inundate a human user in sets of procedures that they can no longer control, that are beyond them. These systems can be equipped with a psyche similar to the human psyche.

That is what this book intends to show: how the architecture of a human psychic system can be structured in an organizational approach, how a human being generates thoughts and how those thoughts then become what they feel; it then aims to show how and with what types of computer component this psyche can be transposed to transform it into a computer system that expresses an artificial consciousness. Thus, we will see how the unconscious, preconscious and artificial consciousness are structured and organized, and how all of that is brought together, with respect to information and energy, with a fourth instance: the organizational layer.

The model of the human psychic system that we will present is founded on an approach that unifies both the bottom-up and top-down approaches. The bottom-up approach considers the system to be made up of many small, highly connected parts and asks how it generates representational forms concerning the sensation of corporeality and especially the representation of symbolic evaluations of real-world objects at very high linguistic and conceptual levels. The top-down approach begins from ontologies of knowledge about everything we know how to represent cognitively and asks how to define the hierarchies of systems that express all of the categories of this knowledge from all points of departure. The unification of these two approaches is organizational and amounts to developing a system that deploys the same kind of morphologically and semantically structured components that define both foundational forms as well as those of great conceptual scope, and which ensure – especially on their own – control over multiple levels like an organizational layer.

And finally, we will see that the development of a model of the artificial psychic system by substituting the human psyche is a scientific approach that precedes building a technology for autonomous systems, and adopting a constructivist and organizational view will allow us to clarify certain characteristics of the human psyche. Science cultivates knowledge that can be shared with all disciplines and also makes it possible to ask ethical questions about its achievements. The development and subsequent exploitation of artificial psychic systems that are equipped with intentional consciousness must necessarily raise questions concerning potential uses or even the justification of a decision not to build such systems. Therefore, the ethical question concerning the potential applications of artificial consciousnesses must now clearly be asked.

.

1

The Organizational Architecture of the Psychic System and the Feeling of Thinking

We are going to present an architecture of the human psychic system by adopting an organizational path that considers the psyche as a highly dynamic idea-generating system that operates continuously at different rates and structures its components on several scales to generate forms, stable for a very short time, that will be understood as the forms of thoughts. In such a framework, the question is how should such a system, made up of multiple active components on multiple scales, be designed so as to permanently produce perceptual and ideational representations of the things of the world using its abilities of naming and language abstractions? We should take into account that the system generates representations of multiple things at multiple levels and in multiple situations, allowing the human to understand reality so that they can act with a high degree of behavioral autonomy. The dynamically, spatially and temporally organized conception of representations will then be the major characteristic of the system, which is, in the end, a generator of complex constructions, usually intentionally, with highly dynamic memorizations. And we will show that the understanding of mental representations always takes place in a specific setting that brings together the psychic system's instances given certain characteristics, which we will call the mental landscape of the psychic system.

We are going to propose two models. The first model will be based on the components that carry meaning, the dynamic union of which defines the characteristics of all thoughts generated by organizing itself by means of specific elements of control. The second model will bring together the components of meaning with those of control in a unique expression that will then be morphological. The second model will represent the generative use of continuous thought-generating constructs made up of multiple aggregates of neurons connected by multiple dendrites, which produce active, emergent conformations so that the system can feel them for itself, based on a highly specific system of self-control.

1.1. The problem of the study of thought

We approach the design and generation of thoughts by taking an interest in the precise architecture of the psychic system. We are speaking about the "psychic system" and we will therefore adopt a dynamic systems modeling approach. But is it common to consider that which effectively generates thoughts as a system? In this domain, the word "system" is often troubling, because it implies – to those who are unfamiliar with dynamic models and their morphological characteristics – a reduction to mechanical and automatous features, which is obviously not acceptable in the case of the psyche. Furthermore, the position of considering the functioning of the generation of thought as that of "some type of system" is unacceptable to those who have the ability to think with immanent features engendered by an infinite source.

We refer to **idea representation** as a form of experienced thought concerning any subject. The brain continuously generates such representations by producing a series of themes of varying duration, some almost instantaneous, others whose duration depends on an intentional focus on perceived or defined subjects.

When we consider the generation of thoughts as the output of a system, we must necessarily situate the model on a certain level that cannot be reduced to the cellular level, which is the level of the minimal physical substrate. We should assert that this system is limited with respect to its effective operational components and its potential for action and interaction, even if these limits are extremely large. We should take into consideration that this system emerges with a certain form, but develops and grows in size and organization in accordance with what is permitted by its architectural process. It continually modifies itself as it is used, and almost continuously, although at different speeds, produces idea representations with finite but multiple characteristics from its emergent states, which lead to behavioral effects ranging, for example, from movements to spoken and comprehended speech. It is an organizational system that modifies its morphology in its running, that sometimes deteriorates and that, in the end, dies with the physical host that shelters it, the human being.

This type of thought-generating system will never be a conventional state-based system, with an initial and a final state for each thought produced; this type of system would be reductive and even absurd in this case. Instead, it would be a system that is continually formed from an ensemble of active dynamic components with variable lines of potentiality and increasingly experienced emergent representations. A very organizational specific, high-level set of processes that imposes multiple constraints is required to arrange the components of the system and to transform it into an organization that will be conscious because it is experiencing the generated thoughts. A conscious event is therefore an organizational act, strictly effective for the set of components constituting the system, which puts them into a particular global state that is able to be experienced. And such an act, which does not occur by chance, must have a more or less precisely predetermined target; it has a duration, constraints, a scope and it has a global substrate at its disposal as the natural result of the operation of the system, which engenders continuous learning and development.

We assert that the generation of thoughts is the organizing process performed by brains when they are functioning, which we will refer to generally as building **experienced perceptible representations** concerning a great number of things in the world. This is what is usually referred to as "moments of experienced consciousness". The notion of representation that we will use here is that of a complex and completely dynamic appraisal of a constructed form, which *can be taken as* its targeted object, which is, itself, a particular thing that is understood by the system. We will refer to C.S. Peirce's triadic signs to clearly understand the meaning of the verb "to be taken as" that we are using here [PEI 84].

This kind of thought-generating system is obviously very difficult to conceive; it is completely different from a mechanism that correlates its output with its input and that operates by passing through a series of predefined states, such as in a stateful system. But it is still a system; in fact, it is a system of systems made up of multiple, strongly interconnected, dynamic processes operating at different levels that are interdependent in several ways and at several spatial and temporal scales. This system, on the fundamental physical level, activates multiple neurons via the activity of their dendrites and expresses the physical occurrence of the transmission of information flow and energy transfer. The system activates and expresses the surges of activity of processes, which we can understand in the computing sense of the term; surges in the process of neuronal actions that are complementary and especially those that occur in parallel. The very important concept of **co-activity** indicates that all actions from an emitter of information or energy modify both the receptors and the emitter itself because of this emission. This is an action that transforms the emitter and the receiver via the transfer of information or energy. The system constructs its own inputs by adapting information coming from the body's senses and endlessly constructs conscious events concerning something that was more or less intentionally targeted.

These specific configurations of the system are always ephemeral and they are produced according to the constraints that are innate or acquired because of the system's operation and the regulation of its corporeality. And these configurations will be – which is the chief attribute of the system – felt by itself, and will experience them while modifying them and memorizing them to use later to produce subsequent conscious events.

By adopting this position concerning the conception of the system, we are situated in the theory of thought generation according to a constructivist approach by proposing an architecture that will allow for its transposition into the artificial, by situating us in the universe of swarms of constantly reorganizing processes, manipulating symbols and measurable values, constructing the organization of very dynamic structures of active elements for themselves and joining forces with each other. This is the standard position for a modeler who seeks to understand how forms as complex as ideas can be represented in the domain of verifiable knowledge and how ideas exist in and of themselves – that is to say, before they are projected into the space of words expressed in language via the production of sentences identified by sounds and symbols using grammars.

So what is a thought? What form does it have, this thing that is so real and so commonplace, so physical and yet, it seems, so hard to grasp? What is this space where it is made, initiated, expressed and memorized by altering the structure of its deployment space in order to memorize and to create others? What is it, this thing that makes it possible for the living organisms who produce them and use them to partially understand the world that surrounds them, to predict events, and, also, sometimes, to question their own existence? How can we explain the scale of that which is thought by the brains of organisms that are so evolutionarily different, and that are also characteristic of its evolution?

1.2. The interpretation of neuronal aggregates

To be able to develop a model of thought generation in a system, it is necessary to precisely clarify the characteristics of the approach as guided by its architecture. Such an approach is based on observations made in neuroscience, which analyzes neuronal activity using photographs of their energy traces, but we must also clarify what must be the architecture of the system, which is principally based on the very organized processing and manipulation of multiple sources of information. There is, in reality, a countless amount of information transmitted at the synapse level, but the understanding of the production of ideas employing words, for example, will be situated at a different level than that of the synapses. We must orient ourselves within the definition of the different architectural levels of the system that generates and manipulates information flows, which must possess traits on the level of knowledge in order to construct dynamic forms that will become the conformations of generated and felt ideas.

The neuronal system operates on the level of production in parallel with multiple neuronal signals, which form, via their associations and aggregations, a very complex unit that can be interpreted as a structure of combined dynamic forms, a structure made up of activities and information exchanges carrying a certain level of cognitive awareness. Every organization of these dynamic forms becomes stable for a very brief moment to form a conceived thought that will be understood. The unit under consideration is therefore the production of combinations of forms of activities, and in fact of morphologies of informational and energetic forms, which combine, associate, converge and modify each other, producing a stabilized, dynamic structure for an instant, which makes it possible for the thought to thus be perceived. This is the physical generation of every produced thought, when we consider thought at its tangible level in the brain.

A thought is formed from numerous meaningful characteristics that are understood, with some characteristics being important and others secondary, contextual, associated or even opposed. The number of these characteristics is important, but it remains finite and understandable on the cognitive level. We assert that these characteristics are represented by the action of significant groups of neurons that we will call **significant neuronal aggregates**, which communicate interactively, and that these groups are interpretable as dynamic forms containing the information for generating the significant characteristics of thought. These neuronal aggregates become active with each other when asked to establish these relationships. They then activate each other at larger scales to form aggregates of aggregates, which will become the form of the expressed emergent thought. It is a question, in the model, of defining these aggregations, clarifying how and why, for what reasons, and in what qualitative contexts they can create themselves.

The consideration of what a thought is at the level of the physical substrate that permits its formation amounts to the assertion that it is an organization of complex combinations of deployed forms that communicate, which implies that all thought is defined by the following considerations.

What is a thought?

A thought is:

– an essentially dynamic, complex physical element made up of energy and information flows from neuronal aggregates that are deployed simultaneously at several scales;
– a dynamic construct using the memorization of the characteristics of certain forms that have already been produced;
– a dynamic construct that expresses itself, that is used by the system that produces it so that it can be experienced, and that only lasts for the ephemeral time period as this conformation in order to perpetuate itself via additional generations of forms that will become the subsequent thoughts, in a continuous process of awakening.

Each thought is therefore a structure created in a series of produced thoughts, with strong reconstructions using forms that have been expressed and memorized. The difference in comparison to, say, a dictionary search structure is radical because there are no permanent components available, but there are reconstructions of forms that have for the most part been memorized potentially in more or less similar forms, using a memory of conformations and not a memory of components, and this occurs with the generation of each idea.

1.3. The function of the architecture of the Freudian model

We can examine five major areas concerning the study of the production of thought in the brain. There is the description of the human psychic apparatus achieved by work in psychoanalysis and psychiatry arising from the discoveries of Sigmund Freud concerning the functional architecture of the psychic system [FRE 66]. There is the work of neurobiologists, with their very fine and measured contemporary observations of neuronal activity and energy flow at the neuronal level, and even at the molecular level. There is the work in the representation of knowledge and reasoning undertaken by cognitive science and artificial intelligence research by relying on linguistic analysis. There are recent discoveries in mathematics and computing regarding the modeling of complex systems, with theories of morphogenesis in complex systems.

And there is also, obviously, philosophy, which offers very profound reflections on what thought is, what it can mean and how it can engage in self-examination [LÉV 71]. But very few researchers have focused on the synthesis of these domains with regard to a precise topic: the organizational understanding of a system having the ability to generate the forms of thought, with the goal of developing a complete concept of the system that produces what we call the experience of perceived consciousness.

We will say that a thought is a **representation** of something precise; it is constructed, felt and assessed in order to be used and reused, and it is systematically engaged in producing other thoughts. We should specify what we mean here by representation, which is not a simple symbolic component signifying a thing, but rather the dynamic construct in the neuronal system that has created and guided a process of assessment with regard to real things that will be expressed and understood. We assert that thinking amounts to generating sequences of such felt representations with regard to the elements of reality that the system can conceive of, with attributes provided by what the architecture allows. Here is the constructivist definition that we propose for the concept of representation.

Constructivist definition of the concept of representation

A felt **representation** is the spatial, energetic and informational generation in the neuronal system of the conformations of an organized surge of a number of elements constituting a precise structure for a brief instant. The surge will appear in the form of an internal organization of neuronal aggregates constituting a spatial conformation, formed at the minimum level by strongly connected neurons themselves constituting connected aggregates. This is a dynamic organization, evaluated sensitively by the system when it is constructed and available to be understood. This representation will be understood upon examination by components representing structural forces trained by multiscale actions on the physical and/or informational components of which it is constituted.

We can say that it can be taken to represent things in the world because of some of its morphological characteristics, which will always be connected to the type of thing being understood. It represents, designates and expresses a real or an abstract thing, by its aspects and its characteristics, and always at a number of scales. This representation, or representational construct, is designed to transform itself into another that is more or less different, which will be the subsequent representation, thereby constituting the flow of generated representations forming thoughts, and which is impossible to interrupt. A representation is therefore not a simple functional state but a dynamic structure of informational forms that is constructed in a continuous and ever-changing procession while it is being consciously perceived.

We should clarify that the process that produces representations contains the following active and organizational components:

1) there are a large number of components of a substrate based on neurons and synapses that constitute the fundamental components whose function is to activate and connect themselves;

2) there are actions aggregating these fundamental components into spatial, energetic and informational forms having certain characteristic qualities;

3) there is an organizational action continuously aggregating all of these forms in accordance with the different spatial and energetic scales in order to build the representation. Each representation on a certain subject has a spatial and energetic conformation particular to the subject at hand, and its conformation can thereby be geometrically described by the constructive and mobile movement of conformations of physical structures having energy and conveying information;

4) there is the action of certain fundamental forces acting on the construct of that representation to extract the global meaning from it with certain important characteristics, principally when it manages to

become coherently organized, which is the conscious act that experiences its representation. The conscious experience of something is therefore a dynamic comprehension that expresses a multicharacteristic sense when the representation becomes clearly understandable, and the psychic system must be seen as an essentially perceptual and self-controllable system that is centralized for the perception of things by the human being;

5) there is a general process that leads to the use or elimination of this representation, which is activated to generate the subsequent representations in a process of continuous activity.

We should note that the process of producing the representation, which is dynamic and mobile on the energy level, influences the state of the representation itself, because it is ceaselessly modified by being constructed from relationships between its components and the targeted intention, and this property endows this process of construction with very distinctive characteristics. These characteristics are instructions for multiple actions that take place and are assessed, as always, on multiple levels. The scientific approach consists of considering this creation from geometric, dynamic and cognitive perspectives, which makes it possible to identify its characteristics in a measurable domain.

Having the idea of something specific therefore amounts to producing a felt representation indicating the aspects of the thing under consideration via an internal construction expressing the characteristics of the thing and possibly an assessment of these characteristics. This is therefore a process of construction and of the feeling of that construction, and it is certainly not a precise state that will be achieved as having been completely predictable. This representation is essentially dynamic; it is a set of activities among specific components designed to produce the representation. This set is, on the one hand, spatial, as it is always situated in several areas of the generating system, beginning with an excitation of aggregations of fundamental components, and is, on the other hand, temporal, because it is deployed and only lasts for a limited time, as it is driven to evolve or to transform by a constant, internal, continuous-layer type of control.

The system generating thoughts in the form of representations must be endowed with the intention to produce them in order to be able to produce multiple kinds exhibiting multiple characteristics. We will now take up the Freudian architectural model in its first version. We will interpret it and assert that its general architecture has four **instances** as follows: an emotion processing center, an unconscious center integrating organizational memory, a preconscious center and a conscious center (see Figure 1.1). More precisely, these instances, which will become the subsystems, are as follows:

1) **The emotion processing and sensory center**, which handles the five senses in parallel and generates different kinds of emotions as immediate responses interpreting physical activity and external and internal perceptual data. Its role is that of the thalamus and the limbic system. This component is very closely connected to the functional elements of corporeality, but especially to the preconscious and unconscious centers. It communicates constantly with these centers to introduce the characteristics of the senses and the emotions in the representations, often by generating representations that are essentially perceptual, immediate and reactive, that is to say, barely conceptualized. It manages the formation and development of emotions in the preconscious and participates in their transformation into felt emotions, that is, into feelings, by being linked to consciousness.

2) The **unconscious and organizational memory**, which situate the impulses and the experience, and which we can consider as situating a memory that will become organizational by engendering it. In this memory, which is potential and which gives form to a universally available substrate, components are exposed via structural and energetic generation, with the memorized events existing in the form of structures of strongly connected fundamental components. This component therefore embodies the structures and the very dynamic organization of lived events by representing an organizational memory in which the memorized components are potential forms with strong relationships that can activate themselves and thus once again become the memorized things.

3) The **preconscious**, through which the structured and active components coming from the unconscious and the emotional center are routed, which shares the controlling components with the non-conscious to create active aggregates with meaning for the representation that is created. This component constructs competing forms of pre-emergent representations by leveraging a morphological analysis of the active components. It will be the locus of control exercised by rational controllers for analyzing judgments, situations, desires, sensations, feelings, etc.

4) The **conscious**, where a form distinguished from the preconscious will emerge. It will be altered in order to be experienced and to be felt, in accordance with a distinctive autonomous process in a specific subsystem at the meta level.

We should note that what will generate and allow a thought to be experienced is a **physical emergence** made up of a complex dynamic structure of neuronal aggregates that has multiple specific spatial forms. We will therefore say that there exist both the form of thought that is experienced in the conscious and the physical emergence that provides the foundation for this perception, which is itself divided into the psychic system's four instances. And we should also note the important fact that what is experienced by the conscious is a procession of unending emergences that are produced at a very fast pace.

We assert that a thought is not a certain language based on a particular virtual dictionary where clearly indicated facts are located, but that it is essentially the operating process of a system that constructs dynamic forms and that holds onto specific memories of their constructs by making the structure of its neuronal aggregates persist. This approach amounts to asserting that there is a level above the neurons, created by dynamic aggregations of the relational activities of neurons (and not neurons as such) that form and deform by allowing for the representation of the characteristics of multiple things of the world, the coordination of the whole of which will form the generated representation. This has been asserted for some time now by Sperry [SPE 80]. Our central hypothesis is as follows.

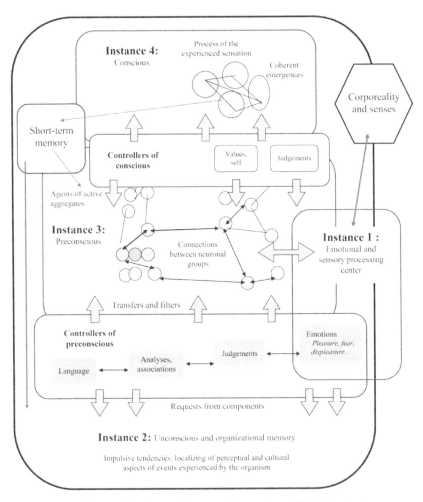

Figure 1.1. *The architecture of the psychic system with its four instances.*
For a color version of the figure, please see www.iste.co.uk/cardon/ai.zip

Central hypothesis of the calculability of thought

The neuronal system operates at the level of neuronal signals and enables, via a large series of parallel activations under the control of a higher level dynamic architecture, for the specification of several parties in relationship and the construction of multiple aggregations of synchronized signaling groups whose global conformation represents a real thing to the conscious because of the correspondence between the permanence of the generated form and the permanence of the understood thing. We assert that these dynamic forms are conceptualizable in a process domain with a highly appropriate architecture for controlling activities.

We can now expand on the precise characteristics of the components of the system driving its dynamic running, which will then make it possible to clarify under what control the system itself is operating.

1.4. The specific characteristics of the components of the system using a constructivist approach

In fact, in order to understand the production of thoughts, it is necessary to conceptualize the generation of thoughts by transposing them out of observation by a positron camera, with the precise reasons for their surges, their complexities and their depths, and instead situate them in an abstract space that uses the possibilities of spatiotemporal manipulation of the information that is generated and used. We must position ourselves in the domain of the swarm of processes understood geometrically in self-controlled activities and adapt this notion of processes to our particular case. This domain, at the meta level in relation to the molecular and cellular level, will be a specific extension of classic calculability as defined by Turing, which we will develop later. It is relevant to the conception of a system that endlessly rewrites uncountable programs with dependent functions, in accordance with certain rules, and which is not content to simply apply previously written programs in the proper order.

To approach a synthesis of models in such different domains, we must first dive into and clearly understand the four domains that were previously mentioned. That is, we must resist the basic tendency, so common today, to isolate the disciplines to make them into fully sealed fortresses. We must be multidisciplinary, we must rethink all of the results and all of the models defined in the disciplines by placing them in a new light. This will allow us to adopt a unifying constructivist attitude. Now, to understand consciousness, we must look into a new class of systems architectures that are capable of self-organization with intention in comparison to their continuous informational inputs and their internal products, by managing parallel operations, and especially by allowing them to experience their products. We must find the keys to control a very complex spatial and temporal organization of a multitude of components that are constantly reorganized, and which intersect with an information flow coming from the sensors that interface with corporeality [BRO 17]. We therefore assert that real thought is the fundamentally dynamic product of a system that never stops building and rebuilding the forms of activities by using its neuronal actions. Clarification of what a form is in such a system is as follows.

The notion of form

A **form** will be considered as a specific construct of components that will in this case be dynamic neuronal aggregates with cognitive meaning and that correspond to combinable aspects, which are actions, connections, separations and flows that modify themselves through collisions and turbulence. All of these components can be defined in a specific metric and cognitive space to constitute a dynamic set having multiple aspects. Such a form will therefore be a geometrically growing set in a metric space where projections, distances, connections, separations, expansions and attractions emerge.

Let us now clarify what we mean here by **system**. The most common notion of a system corresponds to the reactive system. A reactive system might be considered as a black box that always reacts to inputs in the same way to produce an expected result in response. This notion transposes that of the set of well-defined functions representing the system, where this is the calculation of a set of functions defined during construction that do not vary, unless an external user explicitly requests it. We are going to define the idea of a system using a **constructivist approach**, suitable for our area of study, which will be different and much more fit for our purpose.

Definition of a system with a constructivist approach

A complex system with a constructivist approach is a fundamentally dynamic finite system that is open to its environment and that is delimited by a membrane. It is made up of clearly identifiable fundamental components, which are physical, energetic and informational, and which, through their actions based on constant exchanges of energy and information, will form layers of activities at multiple levels that are more or less correlated. These layers will be highly variable and will always be connected to each other to form a whole whose effects will lead, by distributing themselves via feedback up to the fundamental level, to the behavioral activities of the system: the production of movements, of the naming of perceived events or of highly developed cognitive representations. In such a system, there is no automatic causal link between stimulus and reaction; instead, there is a delayed reaction caused by the construction of suitable representations.

There is, therefore, in all complex systems, an organizational level that is only knowable when it is reproduced in constructivist models. There is a membrane that limits the system, and that filters and alters information exchanges with the outside world [VAR 89]. There are the visible effects of the action of the system on its environment, at the level of its corporeality, which will be, for example, the clinical effects studied in pathology that are present in patients' statements and behaviors [MAR 10].

In every complex system, there are many connected components, but there are two kinds of connections. Every fundamental component is connected to another and can act on another component using an energetic or informational message, or even by force via contact. This relationship is therefore usually represented by an oriented arrow connecting the two objects, which creates the fundamental mathematical notions of relation and function. But we will use another idea of connection. We will consider simultaneously active components in which one acts on another to establish a connection that will be concretized and reified for a certain period of time. The existence of this relationship will simultaneously modify the two communicating components using a dedicated organizational attribute. The rule will therefore be that every relationship of this type, of one component with another, will modify the receptor and the emitter in a temporal process that is not a straightforward effect of force at a distance. A situation of evolving, structural interaction will also be created with, in the end, *three* objects: the two active objects in active relation, and a new object formed by these two objects and their objectivized, reified relationship placed into a situation of organizational coactivity. We assert that the two objects have become **coactive**. This notion of **coactivity** will be fundamental in our model, by specifying the creation of an active and modifying relationship between the linked components, where the connection is more than a union or the action of a force. We should note that the neuronal aggregates are sets that are coactive with each other.

Coactivity between components

Coactivity in a complex system is a reified relationship of exchange of energy and information between components, leading to the processing of this information with effective informational transfer. This informational exchange modifies the behavior of the state of the components in play and creates a new component that reifies the creation of the relationship. This concept inhabits a different level than the idea of interaction between neutral components and is specific to complex thought-generating systems.

Coactivity means that the establishment of communication between different components implies that the emitter will be modified by its participation in a relational exchange, that the receiver is not content to receive the information and energy, but that some of its functional characteristics will be modified, and that the existence of the creation of this relationship will be, in a sense, reified via the modification of the potential relationship between emitter and receptor, and becoming (if it did not previously exist) a new component at the level of the relationship between the components. It is clear that the problem of temporal delays affect this process, and that these three modifications are not simultaneous, but depend on the emitter, the receptor and the relationship between them in their contexts. We say that components that are coactive between themselves, or that modify themselves by their operations alone, are **proactive**. Thus, the self-activation of such proactive components leads to their modification, and we should consider that they are not permanent structures since they never stop altering the characteristics of their structure.

By extension, this type of coactive link will be generalizable from groups formed of numerous components to groups of groups, forming complex and coactive conformations that are meaningful to the co-operative behavior of all of the groups of components. We will therefore consider systems with such coactive relationships at all of their structural levels. This type of relationship is not really used in the mathematical domain of functions, where the application of a function does not modify the source component nor the function itself, but is either applied or not applied, as it is from a different domain than the source and target components.

In this definition of a complex system with components in relationships of organized interaction, there is an identifiable substrate, though primarily there is a relational activity that produces dynamic states and the goals of the system, compelling the components to act so that the system behaves as it should. Our goal will therefore consist of clarifying this relational level, which will constitute the system's essential activity, and which cannot be reduced, using predefined deductions, to the symbolic domain.

To understand the problem of thought generation as the operation of a system, it will therefore be necessary to define at least two highly coactive systems, and a new concept of state:

1) there is a **substrate system**, whose architecture and properties will define all of the functionality at the physical, energetic and informational level, and which will make it possible for a second system to exist, the thought generation system. In the case of the brain, this substrate system will be made up of groups of neuronal elements in activity and in relation;

2) there is a **morphological activation system**, which is a system above the substrate system, and which consists of the organization of

the individual energetic and informational activities that deploy themselves in the architecture of the substrate system. This system perpetually uses, structures and organizes the activities of the substrate. It therefore concretizes the substrate's activities. It is a multilevel system of control over the substrate system;

3) the morphological activation system produces, through the expression of the dynamic and geometrical characteristics of the activities in the substrate, and therefore through the characteristics of its conformations, the instantaneous emergent states, which will be called **morphologico-semantic states**. These are extremely ephemeral states that are mental and tangible representations regarding things in the world, thus connecting each multilevel morphology to the meaning of a specific thing.

We emphasize that the concept of morphology that we are using is one that can be applied to a dynamic domain. It refers to the form of the active movements of components in very variable aggregations, and it is different from the idea of the physical form of an organ or an observably real thing. Our definition reproduces that of Thom [THO 94]. A **sensitive idea representation** will therefore be a largely dynamic spatiotemporal construct expressing the characteristics of the activity of the substrate and representing through the dynamic form of its internal communications activities, a thing relating to past or present reality such as an object, a landscape, a person, a word, a concept, an impression, an event or a feeling. These constructed emergences, possessing multiple characteristics that continually vary, are experienced and perceived by the system itself, in accordance with the properties allowed by its architecture.

The end state of such a system is therefore immobility, that is to say, death. It is therefore not a system equivalent to a state machine, as complicated as that may be. We should specify that the state of such a system, that is to say what it expresses through its internal conformations, is of a morphological nature, that of a dynamic, endlessly changing form, a complex morphological conformation that can never be reduced to a symbolic characteristic. A symbolic characteristic can indicate an idea, but without ever making its numerous aspects explicit. We can come closer to an idea about a precise subject by engaging in a long linguistic investigation, such as those undertaken by psychiatrists analyzing the reasons for specific distinctive utterances by a patient, but the idea is a form that exists on a different level than the one of symbolic structures at the level of the letters that form words.

So, faced with such an idiosyncratic system, it is necessary to ask three questions to which it will be necessary to respond precisely:

1) How is this "intentional and perceived thought-generating system" organized such that it will operate and produce through its operation representations that **can be taken** as the things in the world that are experienced by the system itself?

2) How are the highly variable and very complex representations produced by this system made, and what are their domains of existence and the characteristics of their connections to real things?

3) How effective is the system's operation, what qualifies as normal operation, and what are the possible dysfunctions leading to failures?

We have previously presented partial responses to these three questions [CAR 12], but we will here deepen our approach by situating ourselves in the constructivist domain of systems that are constantly modifying their organization.

A constructivist approach to the notion of thought

A thought is a morphological representation that is constructed and that unfolds through time in the form of organized sets of energetic and informational processes in robust interaction. It is a representation that is experienced and perceived in a distinctive way by the system that produced it, which refers to real things through the durability of its forms – their characteristics, their aspects, their modes and their values – and that can take shape through measurable classifications of the behavior of the components that cause it to exist and that compose it. The minimal state of a thought is the factual designation of an isolated thing that has been grasped by the senses, and the most complex state is the pure categorical creation of an abstract event in an existential situation within a framework of open questioning.

By asserting that a thought is the result of tangible and experienced intentional representations, we situate ourselves squarely in the domain of the knowable, and we even can add that we situate ourselves in the domain of that which can be constructed in a calculable manner. We can now propose a first, fairly intuitive, definition of a thought-generating system in a constructivist approach, that is to say a brain in operation. A thought-generating system can be seen as the coactivity of three strongly dependent subsystems:

1) a first subsystem, at the substrate level, formed from a large number of dynamic components in frequent communication, with clearly identified and evolving structures;

2) a second subsystem, at the morphological level (above the previous subsystem), managing the coactivity of the actions of the components of the substrate at multiple levels;

3) a third subsystem initiating and perceiving the generated, multilevel, morphological representations by inciting these representations to produce new forms and by making them memorize themselves in new certain forms of the organization of the substrate elements and the elements of morphological control. This third subsystem is the conscious, which generates intentions and which feels.

The three subsystems are highly dependent and share components. The experienced representations stand in for things in the world that can be understood by the system via the senses and its memory.

We can define the formation and activation of memory according to a constructivist approach. We should clearly consider that the neuronal aggregate is not simply a reactive physical unit, but that it is a system that adapts to its environment and to its changing internal structure, which renders it autoadaptive. This point of view is opposed to that of the reductionists, who only want to see the functional reactivity in the systems.

To clarify this property of autoadaptivity, we will introduce the idea of the **preaggregate**. A preaggregate is a structured and morphological component of a neuronal aggregate enabling the definition, at the time of its activation, of a specialized characteristic defined structurally by the aggregate. It is an opening estimate of what the aggregate usually indicates, which will require the deployment of specific actions that will be interpretable by some aggregates but not by others. This will manage the flow of specific connections between particular aggregates and will lead to the specialization of their functions. We should also specify that there is an organizational level for each aggregate that depends on its context. The requests that it receives compel it to activate certain preaggregates, and this activation enables the production of the refined organizational conformation of the generated representation. We must therefore assert that there exist fundamental components in the neuronal aggregate that are adaptive, in the sense that they interpret contextual data and either activate and send information or do not activate. The idea of information in the neuronal system is based on this.

Information in the neuronal aggregate

We can say that all information entering or leaving the neuronal aggregate is an adaptively coherent flow. On the one hand, it is the instruction sent to the components of its organization through the understanding of the components of its context so that it produces a selective action based on the processing of all of its data and reconfigures itself. On the other hand, it is the flow of instructions that the aggregate sends via the synapses and the selection of molecular, energetic, electrical and magnetic means to the aggregates in its context to indicate its behavioral tendencies and to thus increase the coherence of the aggregates' organization. This type of information is an instruction in the form of an informational flow in order to achieve coherence in the system.

This information, which exists in the form of a coherent flow, is **self-adaptive information** in the sense that it represents the act of selecting molecular, energetic, electrical and magnetic activities in order to use them as an instructional vector for the actions that the receptors should undertake by making them react. It truly is information since it is a choice of action indicated to the receptors, and without which the system would operate randomly or reactively, which is absolutely not the case.

This kind of self-adaptive action by an entity having a fundamentally significant characteristic in the system is precisely that of coactive software agents in self-organized sets, upon which we will elaborate in Chapter 2 of this book. Furthermore, it would often be helpful for computer scientists to take this idea of self-adaptive information into account, which is formed by the reification and the consolidation of the physical requests in a complex system and not by the dispatch of prewritten messages subsequent to the action of a formal analytical process of the situation in a controlled system.

We can now focus on the system's memory. As usual, we will consider the working memory, semantic memory, procedural memory and episodic memory. This classification is functional and is not our concern. The problem is how is memorization accomplished in a neuronal system? And here, the operation of neuronal aggregates will be critical. The aggregates are formed initially for memorizing the characteristics of things that the senses have comprehended. Each aggregate is a component that stands in for a specific characteristic, and the thing that is memorized is necessarily made up of multiple aggregates that must be organized together to form the representation that will be the perception of the thing. We assert therefore that the aggregate is the fundamental component of memorization by storing certain aspects of the comprehended thing in its structure and also by maintaining connections with the other aggregates that produced the representation of the thing. And it is quite clear that each recall of the memorized thing modifies the characteristics of the set of aggregates that memorized it, modifies the connections in the organization of aggregates and reinforces or weakens certain aggregates. The memory of something is a dynamic organization of aggregates that modifies itself when used, and that tends to fade when not used for a long time through reconfiguration of the space taken up by the now unnecessary aggregates. There will therefore be many classes of aggregates in accordance with the types of things that are memorized.

Memory is therefore made up of facts that are dynamic, each time activating a multifaceted deployment rather than an isolated characteristic. It is a set of essentially dynamic constructs that we will call **organizational memory**. We can now clarify what we mean by this type of memory.

Organizational memory

Organizational memory is a global and morphologically active organization that is available for all instances and that bases its activity on the awakening of sets of strongly interconnected specific dynamic aggregates that engender the specific forms of the memorized thing in question. These components can remain virtual, can be activated, thereby reinforcing themselves, or can be locally inhibited by lack of use, leading to memory loss. Organizational memory locally restructures itself each time it is used and each time a representation is memorized. When it is requested by the preconscious or the conscious in the generation of a representation, only a portion, formed of subparts, is activated in order to organize itself in accordance with the intention and the subject of the idea deployment that is created to generate the current representation.

We propose a morphological model to represent the organizational memory of an artificial system and we will see that this model can be transposed to the human case.

Such memory is completely different from a database or a dictionary. Each meaningful component is a specific energetic and informational form and, when it is used (activated), it reforms in context based on the request that activated it. This memory therefore contains facets of the components that it possesses and can therefore remember the coactive connections between these components to affect their organized compositions. This is exactly how human memory is configured, where the neuronal network remakes its own dynamic conformations each time, specific to the current domain, to produce a form of meaning that has already been used and that is therefore considered as known, but which was virtual.

To intentionally produce an idea representation, it is first necessary to initiate the process of representation production. For this, an **aim is discussed** as follows.

The aim

An aim is an idea instruction produced intentionally in the conscious that will initiate the sophisticated formation of a representation that will be perceived; then this perceived representation will proceed to generate several other representations to form a coherent set of idea products about a precise topic.

The operation of organizational memory will therefore be as follows:

1) input of an indicative aim coming from the conscious and making a request to the psychic system through a typified idea instruction;

2) request to the aggregates in the context of the understanding of this aim in organizational memory;

3) for each active aggregate in a group, activation of the appropriate and coherent preaggregate through information from the aim, which will then behave as a local information launch point for the other aggregates with which it usually communicates;

4) reinforcement of the connections between appropriate preaggregates and formation of an organization of relevant aggregates, with dominants and subordinates;

5) coactivation of each group of active aggregates and disengagement from the global organization through the organizational memory;

6) emergence of this organized group as a known form to be used depending on context to produce the representation.

A very important point about a thought-generating system is that it must always function with tonality, that is to say, by assessing each represented thing by situating it in the current emotional, tangible context and so on for each element of each generated scene, thereby developing a context that allows for subjectivity and rational disposition with intentionality [MAR 08]. For this, the system's organizational memory, representing its experience, cannot be a simple database or a knowledge base; we must go beyond the usual models.

We now must clarify the general architecture of a system that generates thoughts by defining the controls.

1.5. The systemic layer and the regulators

We therefore assert that thought is the largely dynamic product of a system that never stops constructing and reconstructing the forms of activities by using its extensive potential neuronal actions. This requires an architecture with general operating characteristics that must be reified in this architecture. This activation component does not exist in the Freudian model, which is a very elegant cognitive approach but is not a constructivist approach. We assert therefore that there is a fifth architectural instance beyond the components of emotion, the unconscious, the preconscious and the conscious, a component that is essentially stimulating and that generates the synchronized control of the activities that produce apprehended conscious events. This instance is the **systemic layer**, which is the fifth instance in the psychic system. It has the following characteristics:

– the **systemic layer** is the dynamic component that produces, through motivational control, the thoughts of all of the system's components at every level (including the other instances), in order to put them into coherent activities and to furnish a representation for the conscious to evaluate. It effectively enables the affect as a training and dominating action established between the unconscious, the preconscious and the conscious while taking the emotional center into account. This layer, which operates without interruption, absolutely continuously, is the major initiating process of the system's activity and is in coactivity with all of the system's components. It should enable the reification of the system's Ego, with its continuous relationship with the external world through the emotional component, expressing the posture of the entire system in the face of reality and of itself.

The systemic layer functions continuously in the human psychic system. It allows the human to be conscious of the duration of time and its inevitable passing, and therefore provides awareness of death as an end. It will essentially be made up of energetic and informational control components operating in coactivity at several levels, allowing it to generate the organizations of neuronal aggregates representing the physical, dynamic, energetic and informational form of the thought that will emerge as a stable form for an instant in order to be experienced. These control elements will be called **regulators**, and we will extensively elaborate their characteristics, their categories and their relationships.

Regulators

A regulator is a controller operating on components, including fundamental components and aggregates of fundamental components, in order to activate and organize them. Some of these regulators will even act on regulators to achieve multilevel control that can exercise control over local controls, which we will call organizational regulators. A regulator is an electromagnetic and informational line of potentiality that can deploy itself in a loop and that operates on the components that it must control. It is the control component in the system; there will be regulators at a number of levels, forming a highly dynamic regulatory space. There will be regulators operating morphologically to propel the inclinations and to generate representations.

Regulators form layers of connections between aggregates to allow them to coactivate; these layers are composed of synapses and chemical elements using energy and information. They are the components of a network that connects the entire system, that links all of the neuronal aggregates and that operates even within aggregates to ensure their autonomy. There are regulators that shape the representation's aggregates into the correct conformations according to themes, there is a set of regulators that enables the initiation of the system's operation and there are **organizational regulators** that control the regulators that only control aggregates. There are therefore regulators that determine fundamental impulses, inclinations and emotions, and there are regulators that set the current aim and initiate the production of the representation. There is also a meta-organizational regulator, strongly connected to all of the others, that will initiate the voluntary production of representations rather than experiencing things neutrally, unintentionally.

These regulator components, this layer of relationships, are absolutely not independent from the aggregates. There is a relationship of coactivity between the aggregates, which will have a certain degree of behavioral autonomy, and the regulators that trigger their activation in certain ways, such that the system is truly organizational, unified and absolutely not made up of different functional levels. And this network of connections will be organizational at several levels, because there are layers at the basic level of groups of aggregates and layers at the level of organizations of groups of aggregates located in specific regions of the brain. All of the organizational complexity occurs in these nested layers and in their very coactive relationships with the aggregates.

The aggregate–regulator coactivity rule

In the psychic system, the components representing the fundamental characteristics of meaning – the aggregates – and the components representing the organization's control triggers – the regulators – are coactive and dependent. There is a systemic connection between these two types of components, which engenders the strength of the developments and expressions of the system, but also their fragility.

We will expand on the highly organized relationship between these two types of components, which characterizes the control system, not as a distinct functional subsystem operating from above, as in traditional technology, but an organizational layer immersed in the regulatory layer. The great strengths and weaknesses of the human psychic system exist because of the coordinated or contradictory activity of the regulators, which enables us to specify the physical origin of a number of mental problems in the psyche [MAR 15].

The general schema of the psychic system's architecture in a constructivist approach with its self-controlling systemic layer is therefore as follows (see Figure 1.2).

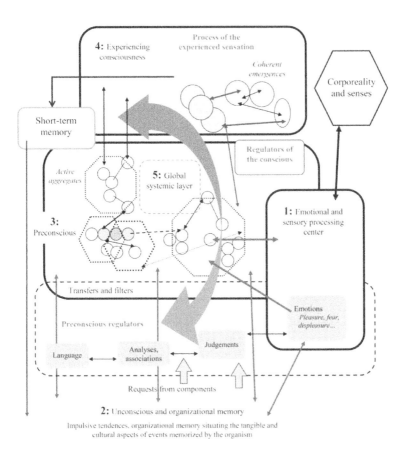

Figure 1.2. *The organizational architecture of the psychic system with its five instances. For a color version of the figure, please see www.iste.co.uk/cardon/ai.zip*

This new architecture requires that we define two things precisely: the regulatory domain and the required characteristics of the emergent form for representing experienced thoughts. We will first explain what regulators are, what they do and how they operate together, in coactivity. We will closely follow a constructivist approach, in which we first specify all of the characteristics of the structure's components, and then all of the control components.

What bases does the control of aggregates and of the entire neuronal organization rely on in order to produce a representation? Regulators are rational controllers of the organization of the coactivity of neuronal aggregates, representing the system's normal psychic tendencies and cultural aptitudes, that is to say, both the impulses and the inclinations, similar to those exercised by a Freudian Superego over the Ego. There will therefore be regulators at the preconscious level, anchoring the effects of the impulses, the abilities of identification and differentiation, of analysis, of abstraction and of categorization, of the tangible perception, and there will be regulators at the conscious level, which will reify inquiry, conceptualization, adaptability, self-awareness, ethical judgments and values. The types of regulators and their relationships are clearly the key to the system's psychic capabilities.

Morphological role of the regulators

> The regulators carry out regulation and control of the neuronal aggregates or organized sets of aggregates; they facilitate the active integration of these components and their placement into coactivity, and they especially modify the tone of the controlled components by adapting them to the current tone of the conscious and sometimes of the preconscious. They therefore provide the cognitive and tangible quality to each emergent representation as well as its value.

The regulators of the preconscious are components that are shared between the unconscious and the preconscious. They are dynamic, of complex structure, and operate at the morphologico-semantic level, allowing, in the systemic layer, for the extraction from unconscious memory of suitable groups of components adapted to the aim and the tendency of expression reigning in the conscious at a given moment. These components are well organized among themselves and form the network of potential tendencies that will contribute the theme, the aspects and the characteristics of aspects at each moment to the perceived form that arises in the preconscious and emerges into the conscious by allowing it to insert itself into the continuous flood of coherent emergences relevant to a sequence of generated artificial thoughts.

The primary regulator for the emotional processing center manages the emotional flows that must establish themselves in the preconscious and that arise from the system's corporeality. It is a very structured regulator composed of numerous subregulators that correspond to a variety of the emotions that may be perceived. It produces an emotional layer and a morphological landscape of coactive aggregates in the preconscious. This dynamic layer represents the emotions that activate each other as centers of attraction, transform themselves, come into conflict with each other and connect themselves to the forms of rational thought.

The regulators in the conscious are directly connected to the systemic layer and allow for its activation and control in order to impose a tone on the preconscious regulators, and therefore to clarify the dominant characteristic of the emergent forms produced by the conscious. The aim provided for thought will be produced by the coactivity of these regulators. The focal point of the current emergence with its connected characteristics and its complexity will therefore be driven by the regulators in the conscious. Furthermore, these regulators carry judgments of value and adequacy concerning what emerges with reality. These regulators form a network that expresses the Ego of the system in its action of provoking perceived idea emergences in a continuous manner. This network is clearly connected to the network of preconscious regulators, normally in a directive manner, and to the structural elements of the systemic layer.

All of the regulators are structured with subregulators that specify them. They form networks with fairly numerous but relatively scalable local hierarchies, since they correspond to the categorization of everything that can be thought, reasoned about, appreciated, judged, perceived, and desired by the system. All of these characteristics have been extensively examined by psychologists and philosophers.

Each of these regulators has the following:

– a specific categorical or thematic domain, which will be limited or extensive, wide or narrow. This domain of action is defined based on the categorization of thoughts that the psychic system is capable of defining;

– a history, classifying them as native to the generation of the brain or else created by learning, such as during education;

– a coactivity, which stands in for the privileged relationship with certain other regulators or conflict with others, which can evolve over time in accordance with the generation of ideas;

– a general scope that will be the morphological deployment of their coactive actions with effects on the sets of neuronal aggregates and on the other regulators. This activity will constitute the morphologico-semantic zone of the regulators, which will have characteristics expressing the potential and qualified tendencies of the psychic system, and which will define its Ego more precisely.

There will be an organization of regulators. This organization will be a spatialized set, with components that will be energetic and active in the current state and others that will be inactive. This organization is formed in the living being for the formation of the psychic system by a meta-regulator with a unique role: this is the regulator that represents the life impulse described by Freud. When the psychic system is constructed, the meta-regulator takes care of construction concerning regulation, which is the central point for generating the systemic layer, and situates the specific regulators that are created in a spatial organization in the form of a geometric sphere or pyramid so that certain regulators will always be dominant and active. Therefore, there is a fundamental impulse in the system represented by a regulator that can take a dominant position.

The fundamental impulse and the regulator of the will

> The system's fundamental impulse is represented by an organizational regulator operating on all of the regulators. This is the fundamental tendency of the system, and it will be represented by a meta-regulator that we will call the **regulator of the will**. It puts the system into tension in order to endlessly pursue its capacity to exist, so that it produces actions and intentionally generates thought forms. It consists of a constructive adaptability impulse that pushes it to understand, evaluate, question and communicate. This impulse can be reduced, put into retirement and can thereby engender an inscrutable situation leading to anguish. This fundamental impulse provides a range of tendencies and specific impulses – according to the profile of the system – that will dynamically incite components of the production of the different types of idea emergences.

There is no death impulse in the psychic system, which Freud proposed in his model. We assert that the psychic system is a system that never stops constructing representations via the fundamental drive of the regulator representing the life impulse, but that this regulator can be rendered ineffective. It can, under conditions in the psychic system in which there is a very strong contradiction between the regulators, find itself unable to spatially arrange the regulators so that aims and clear representations are formed. In this case, the regulators' geometric layer will no longer be established normally in the systemic layer, there will no longer be an inclination to generate a clearly qualified representation, and the system will exist in a state of expectancy and unsustainable emptiness. This is the feeling of anguish, when aims no longer function correctly, when the regulators are contradictory because they are not organized and when each representation that forms is chaotic and compels questioning with no response.

Dysfunctions of the regulators will have major consequences on the quality of emergences produced in the conscious, that is to say, on the qualities and the coherence of the surges of thoughts leading to behaviors. These dysfunctions will have four primary causes:

1) dysfunction arises from weakness in one or more regulators that can no longer operate normally in the morphological space of the regulators and that cannot satisfy their goals or coactivate in a satisfying manner;

2) dysfunction arises from hyperactivity in one or more regulators, which inhibits the action of all of the others;

3) dysfunction arises from informational anomalies in the morphological space of the regulators, which therefore cannot coactivate normally. The flow of information in the psychic system at the neuronal level undergoes anomalies, limitations and local weaknesses;

4) dysfunction arises from the absence of regulators that are necessary for the social and cooperative activity of the psychic system. This does not take into account certain cultural, social or emotional requirements that are indispensable for obtaining reasonable idea emergences.

Based on the duration of their effect, dysfunctions can also be sorted into three categories:

1) they are temporary, in that they occur in very specific circumstances of implementation in the environment, they do not last long and they are not permanent;

2) they are caused by specific kinds of situations having precise characteristics. They are durable and alter the quality of idea production for a long period of time, expressing themselves in several themes;

3) they are permanent, in that they are set off by the characteristics of situations that are very different from the current situation and are always active, and they reflect a profoundly degraded state of the psychic system. The system no longer functions coherently, stably or rationally, and it is globally defective.

Neurons combine to form many elementary dynamic sets for meaning, which are the neuronal aggregates. We have asserted that each of these aggregates stands in for a specific component of meaning, whose energy will be more or less important depending on the importance of its meaningful characteristics in the emergence that is being constructed, and the aggregate will combine with others to bring out its characteristics, which is understood. The organized set of active aggregates will express itself as the source of felt sensations and of all the forms of generated thoughts. Each aggregate, which should be considered as a fundamental unit of meaning, cannot represent a thought; it is only a constituent component that must combine itself with many others. Each thought will therefore be formed by a well-organized set of dynamic aggregates forming complex conformations that will be significant for the sense, the characteristics and the intensity of the experienced thought. In saying this, we assert that each thought has a source that is a multi-characteristic physical form and that is understood in its significant complexity by drawing out a meaning, which is by nature multiform.

1.6. The mental landscape

We will assert that, in humans, there exist multiple specific conformations that allow them to generate mental representations and that clarify their types and their characteristics in different behavioral situations. There is no absolute psychic domain in which a person generates the thoughts they want to, but there are voluntary or involuntary circumstances that will produce psychic domains where thoughts with certain types of characteristics will be generated more readily than others. We will refer to such a psychic domain, made up of organizations of active neuronal aggregates in coactivity under the influence of a network of particular regulators, as a **mental landscape**. The mental landscape is the environment defined by all of the system's instances and is generated by the systemic layer. The idea of a mental landscape is absolutely central and has not been developed until now. It is this idea that repeatedly places the human in a specific frame of mind, depending on their circumstances, mood and condition, and which allows them to think in accordance with the context, by concerning themself with a situation, an action to be taken or a judgment to be made about an understood thing. It is the placement into certain mental landscapes that allows the human to socialize themself and to think coherently at each moment of their life in countless social frameworks. The human being therefore has different domains of freedom of thought that they deploy at certain times, under certain conditions, and in which they think about certain things with certain characteristics.

The mental landscape

The mental landscape is the specific dynamic conformation formed by all five instances where layers of neuronal aggregates are active and where active regulators ensure control through coordination. This is what the systemic layer produces by deploying its consolidation through all instances to produce mental representations according to specific themes that are emblematic of the conformations of mental landscapes, so that they can be experienced by the conscious.

There are many mental landscapes enabling the development of all of the kinds of mental representations, but we can define two general categories with differences. When a person relaxes and does not request any specific focus, the mental landscape is made up of what is comprehended by their senses, by what is seen and heard and will therefore be perceived very straightforwardly in a continuous fashion. This is the natural, neutral, straightforward mental landscape. But all activity of focus on a theme or on something noticed thereby deploys specific conformations in the current mental landscape which are made up of a dynamic set of specific regulators defining the affective and cognitive domains deployed by the characteristics provided by the focus. And here, we have the second category of mental landscapes, those provoked by a focus initiated by the conscious. It is in these mental landscapes that the appropriate sequence of representations to be experienced will be deployed. The mental landscape is a constructive deployment that extends to all instances in the psychic system – the preconscious, the unconscious, organizational memory, the conscious – and, with the action of the systemic layer, it is the dynamic system that unifies these instances via the systemic layer and that brings out the particular possibilities of generating emergences constituting produced and perceived thoughts. The problem is now therefore the generation of a particular mental landscape.

Generation of a mental landscape

According to a person's general condition, their behavioral context and their current engagements, specific organizational regulators coming from the systemic layer and the conscious – which we will call **situational regulators** – will generate the specific mental landscape that will unify the psychic system's instances and will coordinate with the active organizational regulators. We can therefore say that, according to the person's level of self-mastery and their current preoccupations, the mental landscape will be defined by situational regulators enabling self-mastery with intentional production of aims and representations with adaptability, or by situational regulators generating a habitual mental landscape that will generate representations with very common characteristics but without any real intentional aim.

The usual mental landscape – when the individual is not focused on any thought and is completely neutral – clarifies what the senses grasp, that is to say, what is weakly recognized in the environment by sight, hearing and smell. When there is an intention to think about something, a mental landscape is immediately constructed, and is a specific organization of the instances – a regulatory layer that enables the active emission of controllers inciting the generation of meaningful forms to produce representations that are in the specific domains activated by the regulatory layer constituting the mental landscape. There are therefore two general levels of thought production: the level of neutral thoughts, vague and straightforwardly tangible, and the level of intentional, wanted thoughts.

A human being is therefore engaged, according to their education, activities and way of life in society, in the generation of several kinds and categories of mental landscapes that end up defining their psychological type. This clearly asserts that the human psychic system develops several kinds of mental conformations defined by education, training, economic and social practices, and all of the normative practices imposed by society, and there is no psychological infinity that allows for the potential generation of any desired mental representation to occur at any moment. According to time and place, a human is psychologically urged by their active mental landscape to generate the kinds of thoughts that come from their own psychological and social history. A human's psychological freedom is therefore relative; it is anchored in their past and practices, and it can be characterized. In order to form very reasonable and clearly defined mental landscapes and to avoid the generation of somber mental landscapes leading to negative results, one must learn how to thoroughly master one's psychological state. This means that all understanding of a person's psychic system must come from the categorization of their principal mental landscapes, the landscapes' regulations and the situational regulators generating the landscapes' production, and not from an extensive bottom-up analysis beginning with the molecular components that form the neuronal cells, which conform to the energetic aggregates which we observe, and in which we seek meaning and relationships between parts. It is therefore necessary, in order to understand the significance of the active neuronal conformations, to take a dual approach that will be both bottom-up and top-down, which is typically a multidisciplinary practice.

We can also characterize mental landscapes according to their scopes, and therefore the extent of the representations that they can generate.

The different scopes of mental landscapes

> There are different scopes for mental landscapes, from the limiting layer, where the regulators only enable the generation of thoughts belonging to a precise and very limited domain, to a completely adaptable layer that makes numerous characteristics explicit, and where all questions are possible, especially questions full of symbolic characteristics. Between these two extreme cases, there exist system-setting layers allowing for passage from one specific domain to another with regularity, which is the usual operation of a stable psychic system.

A mental landscape is therefore a general conformation unifying the psychic system's instances in a constructible fashion, and which includes particular commitments concerning tangible and cognitive information to allow for the deployment and generation of thought at that moment. We can say that it is the domain of all generated thought, and that this thought depends, in its form and its characteristics, on the contents of this domain as an active control. We should clarify that if there are very specific mental landscapes generating precise conformations, there are also mental landscapes allowing for the generation of multiple types of representations that have multiple domains, enabling adaptability toward types of representations that specify the dominant characteristic of all generated thought. In all cases, the notion of a specific domain in a mental landscape is the activity of types of characteristics represented by regulators, the domains being linked by connectivity and not independent: the activation of a domain always depends on the activity of certain others. There are many classes of categorizations of mental landscapes in the human psyche, allowing for the characterization and definition of all types of produced thoughts. These classes of landscapes will represent all of the kinds of possible thoughts, as with the many kinds of language activities that characterize the kinds of utterances, comprehension, attention toward speakers, in accordance with the multiple kinds of feelings and reasonings, different possible questions in different contextual situations, the observation of nature, interest in categories of components, the focus on a working domain, the different feelings, etc. There will be banal, habitual understandings produced by frequently used mental landscapes in specific contexts and there will be the generation of creations in the context of open mental landscapes that are able to refer to themselves.

We can therefore say that the freedom to think about something depends on the system's general condition and its current state of activity, which can produce particular mental landscapes, by relying heavily on organizational memory, which has been shaped continually through life from birth onwards. The freedom to think engages the activity of the regulator of the will that drives the production of intentional aims.

A mental landscape is an organized set of components of the neuronal substrate in space–time using the strength of the regulatory networks operating on neuronal aggregates. This mental landscape allows for the definition of focuses on particular characteristics in the conformation of the representations, by placing certain components from its domain into a hegemonic position and others into a subordinate position, constituting the active operation for the experiencing conscious. Mental landscapes use short-term memory, which contains traces of dominant forms of understandings and which will serve as a local foundation for the subsequent configurations.

During the generation of a representation, some forms appear in the mental landscape that are more salient than others; the associations of high-volume and high-intensity informational forms dominate through inhibition over forms that would be subordinate and that would not express their characteristics in the emergent representation. Emergence is what is constructed as a force in the landscape and is comprehended and perceived by the conscious. The landscape is a dynamic construct able to cultivate the continuous pursuit of themes through the control of the perceptual regulator, which is the regulator that tends to find a focus by proposing it as an aim for the future emergent generation. The great power of the conscious will therefore be to present a series of pertinent aims in rich and adaptable mental landscapes. The aim is defined by a meta-regulator that provides the system with a way of acting on a focused theme. The selection of these aims can be of the same kind for a certain period of time, during which a mental landscape remains in a permanent state, allowing for the continuity of generated thoughts.

Depending on the representation to be produced, local forms activate in the current mental landscape to constitute groups of forms having dominance over others by strongly communicating with certain forms to supplant those that will become recessive through the encouragement of active local regulators. The set of all of these dynamic forms in communication with each other will express the dominant characteristics that lead to the expressed thought, generating an emergence that will be comprehended. The regulators in the mental landscape therefore explicitly act on the forms that they constitute, releasing organizations of aggregates and perceiving the effects, explicitly and systematically, of their meanings. Thus, for example, listening to someone talk requires putting oneself into the mental landscape of listening in order to interpret audible information, including its tone and timbre, to construct the continuous sequence of mental representations representing the word sentences and complete sentences – with their objective and subjective semantic inter-pretations – through organizations of aggregates that change in the morphology of the landscape according to the interpretations of meaning based on the words that are heard. We can say that every mental landscape of the language type is a class that has many subclasses depending on the context between the speaker and the listener and on the type of discourse that is heard and understood.

The important point is therefore that there are two steps in the creation of every representation:

1) there is the action of situational regulators conforming to a mental landscape, and there is always an active mental landscape during a period of activity;

2) there is the action of specific regulators for generating the aim and producing the representation in this mental landscape, which are the construction regulators.

The main types of characteristics of mental landscapes defined by active domains that are more or less important are as follows:

1) tangible understanding of characteristics denoting an understanding coming directly from the senses and producing an emotion;

2) common understandings in the current context that do not cause surprises or preoccupations;

3) syntactic and linguistic characteristics attributed to an indicated object through an understanding of auditory or visual perceptions;

4) denotative characteristics of a thing in the world indicated by a voluntary, tangible understanding or by inciting that memory in the context of reflecting on a theme;

5) characteristics of adaptability and questioning about something understood to be important at that time;

6) characteristics of closure about dominant motivations using memory and internal language;

7) characteristics given by the continuous action of tensions and the psychic climate of the moment that qualify the current landscape.

There are obviously a large number of kinds of mental landscapes and their characteristics have long since been specified in psychology (and other disciplines) in the domain of research concerning the determination of tendencies of thought. We can assert that, in animals, evolution has formed types of mental landscapes linked to different senses, allowing for the representation of components specifying the animal's situation in the contexts in which it habitually finds itself so that it will behave for the best. And, through evolution, the neuronal system has become more complex in some animals by achieving an organization of and for itself, by organizing general classes of abstractions of the classes of available tangible mental landscapes. This has led to the creation of new classes of landscapes that are very important in humans, which will be complementary to primarily tangible aspects. There has therefore been a deployment of this new type of mental landscape to memorize and manipulate abstract forms in the available mental landscapes that are simply tangible, with the creation of domains of definition and usage of abstract symbolic forms in the form of aggregates of naming and manipulation of these internal abstract characteristics. Thus, abstract domains and domains of linguistic generation have been created, with classes of mental landscapes of a specifically linguistic type in humans, in whom this aspect of mental landscapes has become primary in the psyche, ensuring its social and cultural expansion.

The idea of a mental landscape leads to thoughts about territory and about the domains that humans travel through and analyze during their lives. But humans must move voluntarily into domains that are new to them in order to explore them and to become involved in them. And it is not certain that this is a common occurrence in the life of today's humans. Following P. Sloterdijk, we can be led to think that our existence is primarily made up of repetitions, most of which are of a purely mechanical nature [SLO 11]. This would involve a more limited characterization of the mental landscapes that are therefore constraining, in which the characteristics of the representations that are generated simply refer to common cases that thereby repeat endlessly.

In fact, all mental landscapes are generated by situational regulators that provide the impulse to activate specific components in the available dynamic layer. There are many of these regulators, which form a dynamic set in the systemic layer and which select situational regulators that become dominant and activate the domains of the instances in the psychic system – including organizational memory – to produce the dominant climate that will correspond to generated thoughts. In the case where the conscious is clearly oriented toward the expression of its will, it can impose the type of situational regulator; if not, the mental landscape will be of the current, usual kind, with characteristics that have permanence.

The mental landscape that generates hegemonic situational regulators is a dynamic conformation, and we can regard it as having seven general dimensions, three in space, one in time, one for energy, one for informational intensity and one for meaning, where each aggregate has a form and energy, and which dominates or is subordinate depending on certain connected forms. This set represents the multiple characteristics of every produced thought: subjective and emotional characteristics, cognitive characteristics, general bodily impression, an image of the surrounding world and of its context, linguistic aspects, specific aspects on the theme of the generated thought, etc.

And the term landscape is not insignificant. The relationship we can assert between the idea of the earthly landscape and the mental landscape characterizes a relationship of organizational correspondence between all of the things that are organized in our world, even if the spatial and temporal scales are very different. Thus, the comprehended observation of a natural landscape amounts to placing oneself in an observational frame and constructing multiple neuronal aggregates representing the characteristics of the forms and organizations of this real landscape, specifying that certain components are focused on their aspects, their contexts, their proximities and their distances from other understood things, and also their brief linguistic designations.

There are many categories of mental landscapes in the human psyche that are constituted through the use of the senses, common social practice and the accumulation of the events of social and professional life. This determines the classification of psychic types, which can be initially defined through types of observed mental conformations and further defined using imaging in neuroscience. There are general mental landscapes establishing personality types, there are local landscapes like those characteristic of pleasure or distress, of all the emotions, reasonings, fear or attraction, etc. There is clearly a strong distinction between the mental landscapes of children and those of adults, since landscapes are made up of forms and different conformations. We should note that the psyche allows for the creation of new abstract landscapes based on a landscape whose structure has been memorized, thereby demonstrating its adaptable context.

Mental landscapes are activated by situational regulators. Some of these regulators express the temporary will of the conscious and the need to activate a certain type of landscape when beginning to think about specific things. Other situational regulators will be activated autonomously in order to activate and deepen the characteristics of the current mental landscape. There are also autonomous situational regulators that function by understanding information coming directly from the organism's senses that deploy tangible types of landscapes. We should also note that many mental problems are created by the continuous presence of mental landscapes generated by strongly autonomous situational regulators, which do not refer to the individual's real situation, and which thereby systematically provide contexts that encourage the production of specific abnormal representations. There are even situational regulators that generate obsessive mental landscapes that only allow for very specific kinds of mental representations. We should clearly state that the psyche's pathological characteristics are not simply determined by what a patient says, but by the mental context in which those things are said, and that these contexts are mental landscapes. Marchais and I have previously published on this topic [MAR 10].

We should also state that future autonomous systems equipped with artificial consciousness will be able to communicate forms of thought between themselves by using continuous WiFi transmissions, thereby achieving the computing equivalent of telepathy. We will see this in Chapter 2.

Every human psychic system is therefore a set of regulators that controls a layer of components simply carrying the memory of the individual's life; this memory is organizational and cannot be reduced to accessible, passive components. Its operation amounts to the activation of meta-regulators that encourage the situational regulators to create an active mental landscape, which then cause the intentional regulators to activate, in order to generate the theme of the representation that will be constructed by the local regulators in the layer. Then, the proposed representation will be analyzed and understood by the regulators in the conscious, which we will see.

1.7. The feeling of thinking and the general organizational principle

The human being perceives thoughts, experiences them and can only use them to form coherent sequences of thoughts that are subsequently memorized in a synthetic manner. How does this feeling of thinking come about?

Every perceived thought will structurally – at the physical level– be made up of multiple active aggregates that will be organized to constitute a specific dynamic form in the mental landscape and in which certain aggregates will be more intense than others, that is, they will be dominant over subordinate aggregates. We should assert that every felt thought exists on the material level; this is the generating and exploratory activity of a form organized from active aggregates expressing characteristics. This is a conceptual approach to thought that is presented as the generation and manipulation of highly dynamic forms, the emergences of which are produced by co-active processes, such that the feeling of thinking occurs through the manipulation of forms emerging with manipulating regulators that produce the feeling of understanding a thing, a feeling or an idea. We can therefore assert that the brain is essentially a very efficient system for generating specific feelings that are able to express multiple sensitive and cognitive understandings by representing countless conceptual forms – including linguistic forms – through its ability to generate and comprehend forms made up of dynamic aggregates that use energy and information. Thinking is perceiving an emergence in the mental landscape; it is a feeling that is continuous from awakening, whether the emergences are voluntary or simply presented by the senses.

So, what are the characteristics of these aggregate forms that express the characteristics of expressed and perceived thoughts, and how and why can these meaningful organizations be generated? The problem lies in finding the link between forms made up of active neuronal aggregates and sensory understanding of the whole of these forms experiencing the characteristics of what is defined by these forms. We have here a question that must be asked and answered in a constructivist approach, which amounts to elucidating the following points:

1) consider active aggregates with energy and information by clarifying why and how they are active;

2) consider coactive energetic and informational relationships between these aggregates, clarifying why they are coactive, and what the scales are;

3) consider how the set of aggregates makes up a specific organization in which specific components influence others to form a large temporary structure;

4) consider how and why this organization is understood and how it is perceived as being a conscious form;

5) consider how the subsequent thought – which will contain the phases of construction of the components – is constituted, with aggregates that are both similar and different forming a new aggregate.

A thought is based on a construct that is a sequence of generated representations in the current mental landscape; this involves analyzing the aggregates, an activity which is not neutral on the energetic and informational level. Each representation is generated during an extremely short time, and the sequence of representations that will create the feeling is equally short, especially with regard to actions in the body. It is this activity that will lead to the feeling of thinking about something, and we will elaborate on the reason.

Achieving the feeling of thinking about a thing

The fact of being conscious of something, that is, the feeling of thinking about something, is the process of a cognitive and tangible evaluation of a sequence of representations that are aimed or not aimed in the mental landscape, and that can be analyzed by specific regulators that evaluate the characteristics of their forms by modifying them, completing them and partially reconstructing them with sensitivity. A feeling does not arise during the construction of the first characteristics of the sequence of representations, but is produced on the available construct when it is formed with a coherence that renders it relatively stable for a moment when it is no longer producing important aggregative reconstructions. The effective action on the material components – that is, the sequence of representations formed and available for its analysis and synthetic reconfiguration – will be produced in a major, hegemonic state in the entire system, which means that this analytical action allows for memorization so that the process of generating representations will be pursued endlessly through specialization or generalization or even a change in theme. **It is therefore an analytical state of synthetic memorization that allows for the continuous pursuit of representations**. This action is permitted by the specific regulators in the conscious, which are the only ones that are active at that time in the conscious. The mental landscape is fixed, and the form of the representation is manipulated by these regulators in the conscious. This action constitutes the local feeling of thinking about representations, because it focuses all of the psychic system's operation on the action of analysis in order to memorize the representations and to imperatively proceed with the coherent pursuit of the process of generation at a rapid pace. The process of constructing representations is in a suspended state for a very short time with regard to the form under analysis so that it can be used to define a new aim that will relaunch continuous production in the psychic system.

The fact of thinking about a thing is therefore a process that operates for a very short time on the conformation of the representation proposed to the conscious, which achieves its analysis through the regulators of the conscious – which we will call **regulators of the feeling of thinking** – in order to evaluate the characteristics with sensitivity, to complete them and then to produce a synthetic form that will be stored in short-term memory. This is a delicate and partial development of the available physical structure that will be perceived as such. These regulators take control of the system for a short time and are the only active regulators in the conscious and the systemic layer that produce an understanding of the characteristics of the representation. This action modifies the energy and the informational contents of these regulators during the very short cessation phase of the construction of representations, and the analysis that allows for the production of the forms of the synthesis of the representation will be perceived as sensations linked to their characteristics. The end of the process of understanding initiates the immediate production of the subsequent representation, with an aim or without an aim in basic mode.

The experience of perceiving one's thoughts therefore arises from the action of specific regulators in the conscious that will undertake a tangible evaluation by appreciating the morphologico-semantic characteristics of the representation's conformations with a specific sensation. They undertake the synthetic rewriting of the representation and store it in short-term memory, while the system for constructing representations is now available as it has completed its task. It is an extremely brief halting state of the operating process in the system for producing the sequence of representations in the mental landscape. It is possible to experience thoughts continuously while the theme remains the same by producing sequences of generations of representations that are all very similar, without any change in aim and without an event occurring, which changes the theme of the observation, such as in the continuous observation of a landscape or a sporting event. In this case, representations are generated, followed by a brief sensation of the simple representation, not stored in memory, and then the continuous and imperative pursuit of the production of simple representations on the same theme. It is therefore a continuous fixation on a theme without in-depth investigation, without any changes, and with no deep thoughts.

And there is also the state of the psychic system that understands what the senses provide, that is, what is seen and heard in a continuous fashion when the system is awake. In this case, the psychic system does not produce intentional representations with aims, but understands the automatically produced representation in its mental landscape.

Understanding without intentional aim

There is a situation where the psychic system does not produce any intentional aims, even very weak ones, and where it understands and simply perceives what the senses provide, that is, what is seen and heard continuously by producing continuous representations. In this case, the psychic system simply understands the automatically generated representation in the mental landscape that is shaped by the senses by permitting the regulators of the feeling of thinking to simply understand this automatic construct without voluntary modification. This is a locally weak understanding when it is perceived, without memorization, but whose continuous pursuit leads to thought about a general, meaningful understanding. All abnormal facts in this continuous understanding trigger a specifically questioning aim of understanding and also trigger the generation of a deeper representation that is perceived, which puts an end to the automatic process.

We can therefore say that the usual and ordinary state of the human being is to understand what the senses provide, and that they are bound to intentionally undertake the generation of personal thoughts.

The human being has a system that they can use voluntarily to produce thoughts, questions and reasonings by simply detaching from the tangible understanding that unfolds continuously in their mental landscape. We can therefore say that the emotional instance has autonomous regulators that simply generate tangible representations when the regulators in the conscious and the systemic layer have not taken control to intentionally impose an aim. Thus, the system of regulators is clearly organizational and the regulators drive intentions and aims, which then drive the development of the representation as per the aim, though only acting if the regulator of the will activates the intentional process of producing a representation. Then, the regulators of the feeling of thinking will activate and become hegemonic – when the situation allows it – through the inaction of the regulators for constructing representations. This entire process amounts to allowing the production of organizations of regulators to operate in the correct order, which otherwise engender dysfunctions or pathologies.

The act of intentional thought is therefore a constructive analysis of the representation situated in the conscious that is brought about by the aim. It is experienced in a tangible manner as a setting for the cognitive characteristics of its morphological and cognitive conformation while it is available, for a very short period of time, before the process for generating representations picks up again to develop another. An analysis of the conformations takes place: of their semantic characteristics, their reciprocal strengths and their connections, and the meaning provided by these analyses is surrounded with tangible and emotional characteristics, given the emotional sense of the energetic and informational strength of certain forms in relation to others. Every representation – even very abstract ones such as scientific reasonings – is an understanding that will be primarily cognitive, but also somewhat tangible, concerning the morphological characteristics of this representation. We experience with a certain degree of attention, a certain intensity, a certain pleasure or displeasure, or with a feeling that something is either important or negligible. We can therefore say that the human is and will always be a fundamentally sensory being in their behaviors and also in the fact that they think. Thinking is a sensory perception of one's thoughts. Based on what is experienced as a conscious event, there will be continuity of aims in the same theme and the same mental landscape, or there will be a potentially radical change. The fact of thinking is a continuous action of mental perceptions of forms generated by internal sensations, an action which is intentionally modified according to the characteristics of each sensation. The process is continuous at different paces and is tangible because it is experienced.

The action of the continuous production of the sensation of thought is as follows.

The continuous sensation of thought in the psychic system

The sensation of thinking is a process of understanding the characteristics of a completed, analyzed and evaluated representation, with its reconstruction leading to its synthetic memorization and its storage in short-term memory, followed by the initiation of the production of the subsequent representation. We cannot stop producing representations while we are awake; the necessity is imperative, but the intention to produce them about specific aims exists, as does the sensation of focusing on things without any express intention. The duration of the production of a representation is very short, and there is also a period for understanding its expression and its characteristics while the construction process is stopped in the mental landscape, with the imperative inclination to initiate the pursuit of new productions with a potential change in theme. This sequence of produced representations can be unintentional and can generate a continuous sequence of perceived understandings on a single theme, without memorization and without precise interrogations of the representations, which is the case when the intention to think is very weak. But the sequence can be non-uniform, with the expression of the regulator of the will on a representation leading to a strong investment in a theme in the precise mental landscape and the production of corresponding representations, and, subsequently, the feeling will focus on what has been produced, before changing.

The process of perceiving a produced representation with an intentional aim is as follows:

1) process of generating the representation with the action of the regulators in all the instances;

2) definition of the local components of the representation and of the order that will be given to the set of these components: main form, secondary form, classification and the surrounding of certain cognitive forms with emotional forms;

3) **cessation of the production process in the mental landscape and perception of the representation**: analysis of the important parts, subsequent complements given and unification by the regulators of the feeling of thinking, a strong action of these regulators and a feeling brought about by their conditions and their characteristics of that which is apprehended;

4) construction of the synthetic form and cessation of this construction, which is the end of the sensation of thinking about the representation. Additionally, its storage in short-term memory and use of this constructed form for subsequent generations of representations;

5) action of the regulators of the conscious and the aim: imperative inclination to continue the construction process, either through pursuit of the intended theme in order to understand the thing more deeply depending on the intensity of the sensation, in order to differentiate it more thoroughly, or an intentional passage to another theme through rupture;

6) **resumption of the constructive running** and explicit generation of the new aim, followed by initiation of the construction of the subsequent representation in accordance with this aim.

The construction of the representation is a process of aggregation that rapidly attains a form with a degree of stability, which is analyzed, completed and overcome in order to be replaced and stored in short-term memory. This act of construction, analysis and reconstruction of a synthetic form leads to the perception of thought through the placement of regulators into a hegemonic position over a stopped construction process in the mental landscape, which is the action of experiencing that occurs. The fact of constantly perceiving these representations inside oneself that are made and unmade through this act of perception is isolating and produces the feeling of self, but also introduces a very important receptivity to the sense of time passing through consideration of the different time periods of thought events that are completed and the temporal classification of these events [KAN 96].

The memorization of the synthetic form of the representation occurs through an exploration of the mental landscape by the regulators of the feeling of thinking and a detailed analysis of the form of the emergence of the representation, through an appreciation of the importance of certain aggregates as well as continuities and discontinuities in the aggregated forms that lead to modifications to connections. This occurs primarily through an informational process caused by specific regulators, a process that travels through the aggregates, evaluating them and modifying their connections. This altering process is tangible and produces the physical sensation of thinking by selecting and then altering the characteristics of the aggregates by surrounding them with tangible characteristics. We must therefore consider that the associated neuronal connections that form the relationships between aggregates carry not only the energy they need to form, but also the information they need to endow themselves with meaning and tangible value. This information has a chemical, electrical and electromagnetic basis, and can become morphological in highly energetic and magnetic groups in the mental landscape by having more intense sites than others.

The description of this process explains the act of thinking, where it comes from, what it produces as sensations and as a feeling of the self. We have asserted that the system always generates a mental landscape and experiences the meaning of the representation generated in this landscape by producing a synthetic memorization of the representation. We can now assert that there is a principle that living beings drive all of the neuronal systems to produce the feeling of thinking for organisms that accommodate these systems in their brains. We can assert that experiencing thinking is not a marvelous aptitude that comes from elsewhere and that human brains possess, but that it is the expression of the fundamental inclination that all living organizational systems have the desire to preserve themselves in space and time, to memorize the structures of what they are made of, to store in memory the synthesis of the form of what has been constructed and has moved into the past and to use it in new forms to be generated in the future. This is the fundamental principle of continuity and conservation of everything that is organized on our planet, all of life. We will therefore successively state two principles, the first clarifying why the psychic system produces synthetic forms of its representations and why they are experienced, and the second stating that there is a universal organizational principle that makes a living being.

Fundamental principle 1 – the memorization of representations

The tangible understanding of a representation in the mental landscape, which is the feeling of thinking about something, occurs because the mental landscape tends, by its nature, to make itself memorize these representative emergences, to store the generated representation in the system's organizational memory in order to anchor it there in a certain form, thereby making the representation generating system a system that tends to maintain its organizational possibilities and the permanence of its activities. Therefore, there are regulators of the feeling of thinking that analyze the representation in order to summarize it and then to memorize it, and thought is experienced as a result of these actions.

Fundamental principle 2 – the general organizational principle of living beings

We assert that there is a **general organizational principle** in living beings that tends to organize material to constitute components and organisms. This inclination exists permanently in space and time and tends to memorize the forms that have emerged in a structured fashion by conserving these produced forms, as much as possible, in order to allow for more to be organized, both similar and new ones, that are based on them. This inclination is certainly motivational and is absolutely not imperative. It is the principle of existence and the continuous evolution of living beings that tends to be deployed in local space–time on Earth. This inclination applies in the case of neurons to available forms in the mental landscapes, landscapes that are strongly organized and complex, which for this purpose use space, time and the coactivity of the components of which they are made, thus reifying a continuous need for emergences of representations in a dynamic organizational space.

This principle is effectively produced by the uniformly dense organizational tendency in a space–time where we share the same world line [LAC 13]. It establishes a clear link between the organized living being that shapes the variety of life, which is a complex but organized deployment, and what happens in the brain, which is, at a completely different temporal and spatial scale, a generation of organizations using memorized forms to endlessly create new ones.

Therefore, the neuronal system has the capacity to memorize what it produces as experienced representations, which has the effect of giving to the body that houses this system the ability to represent what it has lived through and therefore the ability to operate continuously and rationally in all of its acts. We must abandon the idea of an understanding of the ability of thought that will be primary, superior and coming from a supernatural source in the thinking man. Things are organized, and the human being is an organizational component of the evolving, living being that actualizes their own evolution and innovates, using the memorizations they have created.

1.8. The aim and the space of the regulators

One of the most common ways that the psychic system initiates the generation of a mental representation is the production of an aim, which is the intentional expression of wanting to think about something and generating the sequence of representations.

The aim of a mental representation

The determination of an aim in order to initiate the production of a mental representation with intention is the specification of an instruction concerning a theme in the frame of an active mental landscape. This will be created by an intentional regulator. There are two cases. In the first case, in which the mental landscape is closed and the aim conforms to the type of landscape, we have a **local aim**. In the second case, the mental landscape is open so that the intentional regulator can introduce a thematic instruction by soliciting regulators through strong coactivity; this thematic instruction may solicit the activation of another mental landscape, which will be done by the active regulators. This is the case of an **amplified aim**. The generation of this aim is voluntary in a landscape that is open to the organizational memory and it may activate another mental landscape; it is a question of the explicit exercise of the intention of thinking strongly about a specific thing, which is therefore a meta control that we can refer to as the **mental will**. We have already seen that a specific meta-regulator exists in the conscious for producing this exercise of will – the organizational regulator of will.

We will therefore define two kinds of aims, which will determine the amplitude and the quality of representations:

1) **local aims** come from very local foci in a defined mental landscape, primarily about what the bodily senses provide. This type of aim is common when the person is not focused intentionally on something very precise, instead when they are simply comprehending normal things in their environment or body, and remaining in this calm mental landscape, providing the domain of natural considerations at that time. We can assert that mental landscapes where local aims are produced are limited to the activity of a few sensory regulators, which limits the expenditure of the organism's energy;

2) **amplified aims** are an intentional focus on a specific theme with questions and with significant use of organizational memory. It is an aim that uses internal space by making calls to memorized knowledge or to experienced events that have been memorized in a highly structured way. This type of aim normally leads to the production of a sequence of aims of the same kind, which then leads to reasoning that can be profound. This is the main special feature of the capacity of the human brain.

The intentional regulator must be in complete agreement with the regulator of the will in the conscious so that it can produce the action of initiating its theme among the other regulators of the instances. If not, a contradiction exists in the conscious, there is no coherent aim, and representations surge up from the preconscious that will be perceived in the conscious, even though they are incoherent.

So, it is clearly the amplified aim that characterizes the very strong freedom of thought in humans, who use this kind of aim very frequently. We can say that evolution has enabled the considerable development of amplified aims in the human brain because it has the greatest capacity for using these specific aims, which leads to rational developments of sequences of thought that manipulate multiple abstract symbols. In living organisms, the human brain represents its powerful evolution through its organization, through which the intentional regulators developed intensely to have the ability to deploy sequences of representations that manipulate internal abstract characteristics. And we should note that each aim of this kind leads to the production of representations manipulating abstract characteristics, and that these representations will be subsequently memorized synthetically by creating a very powerful organization of memory. There is strong coherence between the action of these intentional regulators and the regulators deploying the components of representations through calls to very organized components in the organizational memory that contain the structures of abstract components memorizing lived experience.

There are a certain number of intentional regulators, and they are specific to thematic categories. They exist in the conscious and are continuously active. They each focus on a thematic domain and, in accordance with the initiation of the regulator of the will, they coactivate themselves, and one will very quickly become dominant. They call strongly upon the regulators of short-term memory and organizational memory corresponding to their theme, then generates a theme that is a categorical instruction for producing the representation. This theme will be the instruction given to the regulators for constructing the representation in order to elaborate on it, by using organizational memory and the sensations of the emotional center more thoroughly.

The exercise of voluntary control over the generation of mental representations will therefore be done primarily by focusing on the deployment of the construction of the representation on a subject and by opening an adequate mental landscape that may be different from the current landscape. This control will always be done while a mental landscape is activated with certain characteristics that are sometimes inevitable, such as those provided by the visual or auditory perceptual senses and the sensation of the body's current situation. To exercise the definition of a new aim, the desire for control must be applied to the current landscape whose situational regulators must be dominated by the action of the regulator for conscious control. An aim can also be defined in the generation of a simple mental representation by creating a bifurcation with a certain degree of urgency. There is therefore a detailed organization of intentional regulators through which the dominant theme of the regulator expressing the current aim can be immediately replaced by a new aim.

The notion of a regulator is central to this system, because it is what will allow for the generation and the management of the different relationships between the aggregates at all scales and the direction of an emergent form that will be the expressed thought. By managing the scales of relationships between components and also among themselves, these regulators make it possible to define precise kinds of representations and rational inclinations that lead to the production of representations. Therefore, there are ontological classes of regulators that represent needs, desires, the specificity of the will, the action of impulses, emotions, feelings, sociability, the ability for abstraction, speech, reasoning, judgments, the quality of memorized components, interrogations, classification, etc.

The regulator and its ontological classes

We can consider that each regulator of the system is a line of potentiality acting on layers of aggregates and that it belongs to an **ontological class of regulation** and to a specific category.

It communicates strongly with the other regulators of its ontological class to form a coherent and ordered control group.

The regulators are inevitable components characterized by the training and sociability of the individual. Ontologically, they represent the "action verbs", that is to say, everything that is a real or virtual action expressed by a representation, where the fundamental components are the structured aspects of this action scene. The highly coactive set of regulators will form organized, dynamic spaces where they will operate on themselves to modify themselves. It is a type of controller in a system that is self-controlled, whose control is not external nor strictly hierarchical, but occurs in its own organization in accordance with its action. The regulators are lines of potentiality in the neuronal network; they are what brings about its organizational activity.

There are three main levels of activity concerning the regulators, and therefore three main kinds of regulators as follows:

– we regard **structuring regulators** as those that operate on the level of neuronal aggregates, which act on fundamental components in the unconscious, the preconscious and even the conscious in order to control the coordinated formation of aggregates of the fundamental components. These regulators make, modify and unmake aggregates and clusters of aggregates;

– we regard **situational regulators** as those providing the context for the system's activity, forming its current mental landscape. These regulators form the context of deployment for all of the representations;

– we regard **organizational regulators** as those operating on the level of the morphological components of the conscious or of the systemic layer, and which control the structuring regulators. These are therefore the controllers of the regulators. We will encounter regulators, for example, that define inclinations, desires, aims, intentionality and will in the psychic system.

We should note that the structuring regulators exercise their control through a more or less strong stimulus on the aggregates: they incite the components that they control to act in a certain direction, which is their ontological category. These controlled components cannot follow this instruction, and the regulator thereby takes this choice into account. There is therefore a certain degree of coactivity between the regulators and the controlled components, which are primarily aggregates. And the regulators of the three categories are also obviously coactive.

The roles of the regulators

Situational regulators define the current mental landscape, which will be the precise context for the deployment of the representations through the activation of specific regulators for managing the aggregates and activating the components of organizational memory. Structuring-type regulators exercise control by inciting the fundamental components and the structures of fundamental components in the instances in which they manage the activities. They produce the rational structuring of these components and facilitate their insertion and their coactivity by causing the generation of dynamic forms of fundamental components. They modify the tone of the controlled elements by adapting them to the tone that they should execute, by always operating at multiple scales. Another type of regulator, the organizational regulator, controls the structuring type regulators by organizing their control in accordance with ontological inclinations. All of the system's regulators will be coactive, and they will form morphological spaces of action for control through orientative stimulus over the fundamental components that they constantly organize and reorganize.

The regulators therefore occupy three major domains: the domain of the situational regulators, the domain of the structuring-type regulators and that of the organizational-type regulators. The action of every regulator is rational and occurs in cooperation with the other active regulators operating in the same domain. This action occurs as follows:

– every active regulator has an effective theme defined by its ontological class and its specialty in that class. Depending on the ontological characteristics of its active theme, it produces an analysis of the morphological structure of the active components it controls. It releases the pertinent characteristics of this organization;

– then it analyzes, via communication, the state of action and the influence of the other active regulators nearby, in order to clarify its degree of freedom of action according to its specific ontological class;

– it tries, like each regulator in the domain, to amplify or to reduce the action of certain components that it controls by calling other components into activity and, with the help of the associated regulators to extend or to focus its own semantic tendency;

– after acting, the regulator analyzes and memorizes the result of its action in order to train itself, which it does systematically and which enables it to adapt and therefore enables the psychic system to do the same.

The regulators – of which there are always many active in the system – which would otherwise be inert, define a space of action and control in the psychic system.

Morphological space of the regulators

Regulators are the components that control the system's activity at all of its levels, an activity that is founded on dynamic, multilevel control. These are the lines of potentiality of the energetic and electromagnetic network of the neuronal system. There are many functional regulators that directly control the fundamental components, and there are regulators that control these regulators at several levels. There is in fact – and this is the key point of the system – a general morphological space for the regulators, whose variable dynamic morphology will be specific to the aspects given to each of the generated representations, to the intention to generate them and to the way in which they are experienced.

We should clarify that the notion of a morphological space for the regulators characterizes the very dynamic and multilevel manner of exercising control and producing intentionality in a system that operates primarily through the evaluation of communications between its components and on transfers of energy and information. At the architectural level of the system's instances, there are two categories of organizational regulators depending on the instances in which they exercise control:

– regulators operating on the level of the connection between the unconscious and the preconscious, thus producing their own activity outside of any conscious control. This is the kind of activity that Jung proposed [JUN 64]. These regulators will reify impulsive inclinations and memories by organizing the organizational memory and knowledge – including linguistic and abstract knowledge – into layers of landscapes, which will be made up of smaller layers of landscapes. They will also enable the creation of dreams;

– regulators operating on the level of the connection between the conscious and the preconscious, which will be almost completely located in the systemic layer interfering with the conscious, and which will enable the creation and control of the themes of thoughts and the effective exercise of the system's reason and will think about specific things, positioned in the temporal flow of understood ideas.

Let us now clarify the actions of the different kinds of regulators depending on the instances in which they are located.

The organizational regulators in the preconscious and the unconscious are specific controllers for the types and characteristics of the idea constructs that they will contribute in producing. Some of these regulators are specialized, manage organizational memory and extract, activate and aggregate fundamental components representing the memorized characteristics, according to the theme of the aim as well as the structures of the mental landscapes. Other regulators function as representatives for the impulses. They filter and modify the components passing from the unconscious to the preconscious without any control from the conscious. These regulators, which are numerous and highly structured, will provide the unconscious with the ability to act strongly in the construction of representations, in accordance with the components of organizational memory that are activated and transferred within the preconscious. They will be involved in the construction of a new active mental landscape in cooperation with the regulators in the conscious. These regulators will specify the deep characteristics as well as the functional, rational, cultural and tangible characteristics for all generations of representations, from the identification of objects to their activation and designation into plans of action, and will also specify emotions and sensations.

The organizational regulators in the emotional processing center will be general and shared through coactivity with the preconscious regulators. These control components will allow the system to accomplish a particular tangible and subjective behavior according to the context, endowed with meanings and, potentially, depth. There are domains, hierarchies of emotional regulators and an emotional context in mental landscapes and in most representations, which will enable the production of representations having, either directly or deeply, subjective qualities. These emotional regulators are adapted to the body and the typology of the multiple emotions that can be perceived using the body's senses.

The organizational regulators in the conscious will implement the conscious intention and the ability to perceive representations. The regulator of will continuously spurs the system to function rationally and to organize and reorganize itself. The regulators in the conscious can choose the mental landscape with precision. They control the organizations of aggregations that are available in the preconscious by provoking the emergence of the representation through differentiation, with the ability to evaluate the pertinence and the meaning of the representation. Some specific regulators in the conscious will analyze the emergent form in order to memorize it, and will thus generate the feeling of thinking, introducing the sense of the self in the process of thinking, which will be the activity of the regulators created by the conscious. All of these regulators create the system's deep psyche, its ability to want, and its ability to situate represented events in space and time. They will activate the morphologies of aggregates in the preconscious, in accordance with their specific features, by engaging in questioning, adaptability, abstraction, categorization and especially ipseity, thereby guaranteeing the permanent idea of the Ego in the conscious, which tends to experience representations for itself. These are the regulators that provide experienced thoughts with tone and meaning, notably by reifying the concept of the interrogation of understood things by engaging the system's will to produce one or another sequence of clearly experienced emergences, in some situation or another. They will therefore shape the organization of the regulators hierarchically, and they will form a morphology of control. A specific regulator at the meta level (and therefore located in the systemic layer, the regulator of intentionality) will make it possible to define the system's free will. In every case, these regulators will be able to use the preconscious regulators, more or less strongly, through indirect control and especially through coactivity, in an attempt to ensure a certain degree of control by the systemic layer.

There will be major regulators in the conscious, regulators that will analyze and construct in order to make it possible to perceive the feeling of thinking. These are the regulators of the feeling of thinking, which will analyze the conformations of the representation and will extract from each conformation its meaning, its energetic and informational importance, and its connections with others, and will associate each characteristic thus found with a sensation of importance and a suitable emotional characteristic by surrounding all of its extractions with a tangible loop. Each of these regulators will operate via a broad network of dynamic graph-type actions in order to analyze the characteristics of the representation in parallel. They will also use the regulators connected to organizational memory and the emotional center to complete their analysis.

We must also consider that the structuring regulators are incitatory controllers that simply incite the neuronal aggregates to activate, to communicate, to associate, to unite and to form a specific organization in accordance with all of their morphological and semantic characteristics. There will be tendencies to constitute conformations that are complementary to the main conformation, and there will also be contradictory tendencies constraining associations between the regulators in order to maintain a regulator in a position of dominance. There are even tendencies that will tend to isolate a regulator and will put it in conflict with the others. The system will try its best to reduce this via the action of the stabilizing organizational regulators located in the systemic layer. There are also two characteristics that correspond to the fundamental tendency of the self to an outward or inward focus, as defined in psychiatry, which will be represented by organizational regulators operating in a hegemonic fashion when possible. The set of regulators is clearly self-organized and has the means to produce its own organization, to make it operate in a unifying fashion, and to avoid all forms of chaotic rupture.

The desires will be represented by organizational regulators of inclinations oriented toward acceptance or rejection concerning real objects apprehended by the system's senses, or to abstract objects, with the apprehension of the object and the desire together constituting the current representation, and with a certain situation of strength in a mental landscape procuring these subjective characteristics. These desires will drive the system to pose questions about what it comprehends, in a continuous manner, by activating the regulators that represent the tendency to question. There is another aspect that must characterize the quality of the regulators expressing the drives: there are drives for representing space and time completely, and there are also inclinations for symbolizing and for abstracting perceived information in order to make internal objects in the psychic system and to structure the set of these objects. These inclinations will be represented by highly conceptual organizational regulators operating in the conscious and the preconscious and located in the systemic layer to unify the system.

And finally there is the regulator of the will, which is always ready to initiate the organized activation of the inclinations and their actions, so that the system will continuously generate understandable representations. It expresses the inclination to continuously organize the state of the system so that it will generate representations in accordance with different rhythms.

The process of generating a representation in the psychic system at the level of the regulators is therefore as follows:

1) a mental landscape is active and initiates a certain climate of activity;

2) the regulator of the will to think activates the system and orders the activation of the organizational regulators;

3) the organizational regulators of the sensations are activated and activate the aggregates corresponding to the tangible situation of the organism at that time;

4) the situational regulators engage the impulse regulators in the unconscious so that they can coordinate and cooperate with the regulators in organizational memory and the regulators in the conscious in order to establish the general contextual atmosphere of the mental landscape where the representation will be generated;

5) after the unification of the active regulators by these situational regulators, the latter will carefully adapt the mental landscape formed of aggregates and structuring regulators, and supervised by coordinated organizational regulators;

6) the regulators of organizational memory activate themselves in order to activate the layers of aggregates and to situate them in the mental landscape;

7) the organizational regulators that initiate aims coordinate with each other; one of them will become hegemonic and will initiate the aim in cooperation with the situational regulator in the mental landscape;

8) the aggregates become aware of the aim and activate themselves within the framework of this aim, and, through coactivity, they activate other aggregates extracted from organizational memory;

9) the structuring regulators activate themselves in order to activate and control the aggregates of the mental landscape to generate a representation corresponding to the theme of the aim;

10) when the representation formed of controlled aggregates becomes coherent and is no longer developing, the conscious takes

control of this representation, and its regulators of the feeling of thinking activate, helped by regulators providing emotional appreciations of the characteristics and the importance of the components of the representation. The feeling of thinking is produced by constructing the synthetic form for memorization, which is sent to short-term memory;

11) the organizational regulators coordinate in order to proceed with the experienced representation and to lead to the generation of any subsequent representations.

Everything is duly in relation in the psychic system, in a set of layers of feedback and influence driven by layers of regulators, and these regulators are sensitive to the energy of important aggregates, which will thus produce, via the general coactivity, the great power of the psyche.

1.9. The attractors

Regulators that form a morphology for rational control will not be the only controllers in the psychic system. There is also another category of controllers that will have an important role both in the psychic system's creative power, and in the creation of mental pathologies [MAR 11]. In our model, situated as it is in the constructivist paradigm, there is the notion of attractors. Attractors are controllers of the same functional type as the regulators we have already presented, but they are autonomous in the sense that they are indifferent to the actions of the systemic layer as well as the regulators of the conscious. They form a relatively heterogeneous set, because each is equipped with autonomy and a strong ability to influence the system's operation.

The attractors

Attractors are control elements based on the control performed by the regulators. These are control elements of the same type as the regulators but are essentially autonomous and do not depend on the coordinated action of the regulators of the systemic layer. They represent aspects of novel control at different levels

> because they are independent of the action of the conscious. They connect and influence the behavior of aggregates in the mental landscape and the preconscious so that they will adopt, through coactivation, a behavior with a specific morphology and a specific semantic in accord with their own characteristics. They evolve and their evolution depends heavily on both the system's activities and its capacity to dampen them.

Attractors are coactive autonomous controllers that are initially generated in the regulators' orbit without being subjected to it. They evolve and specialize or interpret the roles of the regulators from which they inherit their attributes. Little by little, they will become autonomous in relation to the regulators from which they are derived, and they will function morphologically, outside of global control from the systemic layer and the conscious. These components communicate with each other and characteristically represent the aptitude for autonomy and novelty in the production of representations in the psychic system and in the formation of mental landscapes. There will therefore be a morphological space for the attractors that will alter the behavioral tendencies of the regulators in the preconscious and the conscious through coactivity and conflict by opposing the action of the regulators in the morphological space.

The structuring regulators act to form sets of well-structured components that are functionally very precise in accordance with the tendencies exercised by the organizational regulators. The notion of an attractor will disturb this operation. By introducing attractors that are created in an autonomous surge that is not controlled by the network of regulators, possibilities for innovative, emergent generations are introduced into the system, as well as the inevitable potential for dysfunction. We assert that attractors are lines of influence; they are components that organize – locally and for themselves – the behavior of the groups of aggregates that they control. They tend to conform in a specific way to those components that they influence by altering their organization to adopt a certain tone, to activate them, and to make them coactive by providing them with some specific characteristics and forms that are outside of the rational action of the regulators. These components will generate the emotions and the strong tendencies and will introduce hugely original cognitive components with requirements that are often inadequate to the context. This will sometimes lead to pathologies.

The attractors can have the same cognitive categories as the regulators, but their role is to disturb the rational and deterministic behavior of the regulators through independently controlled actions of will exercised by the organizational regulators in the conscious, which are therefore independent of the regulation exercised by the systemic layer. These control actions are exercised through trial and error, and are outside the control of the regulators by opposing themselves to the latter. These components will allow for the creation of associations that are opportune and outside of rational, or purely rational, comprehension and that are also purely rational between the aggregates of fundamental components. They will be able to create semantically new aggregates via new morphological creation that will be the key to imaginative production and to purifying creativity. In such an organization, creating an original representation will therefore consist of generating completely new conformations and sets of aggregates via these attractors that will lead to original components in parts of aggregates that were previously in conformance with and supervised by the regulators. Here, the notion of the morphological modification of representations achieves its full force.

The attractors will therefore be autonomous controllers that have a variable degree of influence on the operation of the psychic system [MAT 10]. The minimum level of influence will lead to deterioration in certain specific aggregates, deforming them to a variable degree by introducing slightly original characteristics in certain situations. The maximum level of influence will entail the deformation of the organizational memory, of the mental landscape and of the domain of the regulators, which will correspond to an option of destructuration. Depending on the themes and characteristics of these deformations, we can recognize numerous themes from mental pathologies. We can define numerous classes of attractors according to their ontological domains, their breadth of deployment and their intensity. This is work that should be done in psychiatry; we have previously specified the main outlines [MAR 11].

The systemic layer connects the conscious, which, along with the preconscious, experiences and produces reason, allows or prohibits the tendencies and extracts components of memory from the unconscious through the preconscious, which prepares emergences in tune with the mental landscape by constructing them, by aggregating them and by shaping neuronal aggregates. It is through the rational action of this layer that the quality and depth of thought and reasoning is defined, and it is here that we can show that, when the conscious loses its power over the regulators through the actions of the attractors, thought can either generate creativity or can become lost in meandering.

The action of the systemic layer is regulated rationally by a trending control and by regulators corresponding to the culture and required sociability. We therefore assert that the components of culture anchor the regulators and even structures of regulators forming layers of influence in the psychic system. But the systemic layer can be deregulated by the attractors through their autonomy insofar as they benefit naturally from this opportunity for taking advantage of the systemic layer to react with strong autonomy according to their aptitudes. And here, we make use, along with the notion of a regulator, of a fundamental principle about living things that defines two impulses. Every living organism has an impulse tending to focus and specialize operations, and an impulse tending toward adaptability, toward the unfolding of its complexity. These two opposed, fundamental inclinations are both organizational inclinations, not forces centered in physical aggregates but organizational principles. This is why there are two types of control elements in the psychic system that we have introduced:

– the regulators, which structure and act rationally in context by tending toward a global equilibrium negotiated over time through coactivity, and which organize the global state by negotiating the construction of broad, well-organized structures;

– the attractors, which cause the trending surge to unfurl and which amplify local unfoldings, specialized and local, by going outside the rational context and by favoring a type of very active and original flow that is as efficient as possible through this specific action.

It is therefore through the conflict between the two control layers, that of the activity of the regulators and that of the activity of the attractors, which the question of reason in the formulation of ideas will play out. This is how a surge of thoughts will either become very coherent and rigorous, or noncoherent and even paradoxical, all while being apprehended by the conscious experiencing them. The notions of tolerable contradictions, of convincing but arbitrary simplification, of ease and of the loss of exigence, which are common in human thought, will be resolved through the resolution of this organizational conflict that guides all of the emergences of ideas.

The two different classes of attractors, depending on the architecture of the system's instances, are as follows:

Preconscious attractors

> A preconscious attractor is a dynamic element with morphological action that has two instances: on the one hand, a network of action in organizational memory, which is therefore in the unconscious, where it connects and influences the factual components that support it to form a dynamic network, and, on the other hand, a filtering network located in the orbit of one or more regulators that carries out organizational and morphological modifications of the general aspect of the preconscious and the mental landscape. This attractor is always connected to one or more regulators that generate its autonomous activation through their activations, and to other attractors with which it combines to express themselves and to subdue or to inhibit dynamic components in the mental landscape.

The role of a preconscious attractor will be to undertake a certain morphological bifurcation in the area of the active neuronal aggregates in the mental landscape, in the preconscious, and to modify the organization according to a sensitive tendency that corresponds to the expression of its type. The action of the attractor will consist of transferring its specific profile to the action of the regulators connecting the unconscious and the preconscious by modifying their behavior. This therefore completely avoids the conscious, which can only notice or endure the conformations forming the idea generation that will be perceived. It will only be able, in its turn, to activate its regulators to reduce this influence, if these regulators for evaluation demand it.

Conscious attractors

A conscious attractor has the same structure as a preconscious attractor, but it embodies the ability to provide a type of intention and a particular type of tonality to the general process of operating in the systemic layer via the mental landscape. This tonality indicates the intention, the will, and the atmosphere for the generation that will be emergent, as well as the placement in time of what is produced and perceived. It has the ability to control the activities in the systemic layer. It is its own inductor and can deploy itself without taking past emergences into account, thus creating bifurcations of the theme. The morphological space formed by these attractors surround a part of the system's Ego.

The conscious attractors are important agitators. They are no longer generating original representational forms, but are alternators that direct the system toward non-rational idea generations.

In a general way, the attractors are necessary so that the psychic system can carry out a series of emergences under tonality and can specialize, by itself, in the development of well-adapted domains in the scenarios it represents, with the ability to create original representations and to process very large sets of scenarios through specific morphological structures. The attractors are created in the psychic system by a property that is intrinsic to it: the system allows for the creation and modification of the aspect components and the control components. It therefore possesses, in its native architectural structure, generators of attractors. The system creates itself with regulators that manage the fundamental, tangible and cognitive forms and sometimes with native, autonomous attractors that are there to amplify the system's organization. This system operates and develops in a continuous fashion.

Let us examine an example of an action scenario for the attractors. Humans have very strong feelings, and the feeling of fear has a physical and psychic origin that can invade the system that generates representations. At first, during the appearance of the feeling of fear, every rational representation is eliminated and replaced with an invasive representation of blockage concerning a fact or an event and an inhibition of rational thought and well-managed physical behavior. The individual feels as though they are dominated by an event that is grasped in its global form, but which is not analyzed or broken down. This normally lasts for a short enough period of time, but it can last longer when the fear reinforces itself and it can eventually become panic. Then, after the invasive feeling, rational representations return, but with questions that have no precise answer, which therefore leads to rational control by the weakened regulators in the conscious. We can therefore ask whether fear is caused by an attractor that becomes dominant for a moment and that reduces the activity of all the regulators for a short time in order to be active with the reactivated regulators, but by disturbing the aims and representations by leaving behind persistent characteristics of a negative feeling. The conscious and the systemic layer are therefore disturbed by the action of this attractor.

There are native attractors in the psychic system, but the construction of new attractors is always possible, depending on the characteristics of the person's life and the experienced and lived-through ruptures of consistency. A purely mental creation is the effect of an attractor that operates in the domain of the creation of new relationships and new conceptual generations by putting pressure on the components coming from organizational memory and by generating new constructions with completely original associations of cognitive aggregates. These attractors also allow for deep amplification and stabilization as a dominant mode of expression of the important aspects the system has generated based on its values or its fundamental tendencies. In this case, the ability to create and invent will be based on the correct use of certain attractors for adaptability and for a radical modification of the rational limits imposed by the regulators. With this potential for creation, there is great potential for the evolution of the psychic system, which is very powerful. But an attractor can end up in a situation where it has to endlessly resolve conflicts of tendencies between itself and the typical action of the regulators, which runs the risk of amplifying unstable phases. Thus, conflicts between the Ego and the Superego will be represented by the action of attractors under conditions where the conscious does not totally dominate what it produces.

1.10. The generation of a representation

We can now precisely define how a representation is generated using the aim, the current mental landscape and the regulators. The process of generating a representation has the form of an algorithm, but we should again specify that it is absolutely not a traditional algorithm that operates on data, because the operation modifies the elements used and the characteristics of the process itself; sometimes superficially but occasionally deeply.

Once the aim has been specified, the generation of the new representation takes place. The process of the production and the use of a mental representation will therefore be as follows:

1) there is the **initial context** for the production of the new representation, which is provided by the current mental landscape in the psychic system. There are situational regulators that have activated and coordinated the other organizational regulators to generate the mental landscape. This landscape, which is active and ready to tie up the generation of the representation, places the psychic system into a specific frame, depending on the general state of the person and their will, by focusing on a domain or based on their habits;

2) then there is the regulator of conscious will, which **generates an aim** through the action of the intentional regulators, which are coordinated in the domain of the mental landscape and produce an instructional theme that is precise or that presents a certain emotional incentive. Attractors can influence the theme of the aim and can disturb the mental landscape. This aim can be an abstract instruction arising from worry, a desire to specify a characteristic of the preceding representation, a new intention, or a strong tension exercised by a sense of perception about something in the body or the general

context. This incitement takes place above the current mental landscape. There can be **changes to the current mental landscape** by the regulators if the aim is of a different type than the ones the current mental landscape will allow; if not, there will simply be a reorganization of the mental landscape;

3) immediately after the upsurge of this incitement and its placement into the mental landscape, the structuring regulators are activated by the hegemonic intentional regulator, and there is also a strong and parallel activation of the system's fundamental components, which will generate several aggregates and immediately construct a **pre-representation** or several pre-representations about the theme provided by the inciting aim. Each pre-representation is a set of active forms according to the domains corresponding to the incitement, but which are not sufficient to form a well-structured and stable representation. A hegemonic pre-representation will be released – it is more important than the others and will be the one that the conscious will apprehend. This is how the instance of the preconscious of the psychic system is used;

4) when these elementary forms will have been produced in the chief preconscious of the preconscious, there will be the tangible process of the construction of the representation that will be established. This amounts to initiating the operation of the control components in all of the instances, including the conscious, on the components of the pre-representation that are released into the preconscious, taking the psychological atmosphere of the current mental landscape into account to produce, develop and effectively construct a representation that will then be experienced through the activity of the control components. There will be a very rapid, coherent deployment of active forms organized in all the instances where the mental landscape is deployed, which will reinforce the characteristics of this mental landscape, which will have its full coherence. This act of the construction of characteristics in the pre-representation is produced by the actions of the control components, which construct, associate and complete the characteristics by eliminating some of them. Each local act of construction in the mental landscape is produced by **construction structuring regulators**, which provide a form that is organized according to its components, with the

regulators operating in parallel and in coactive communication. The constructed form, made up of multiple active aggregates, is achieved when a sufficient and briefly stable global form is constituted and expresses the reification of the aim's theme;

5) the representation in the mental landscape, which is briefly stable, is explored by the organizational regulators of the feeling of thinking in the conscious, which completes its construction, determines the characteristics and meanings of its form and provides the apprehension of the meaning of its set, which produces perception and the conscious event of the experienced representation. The appreciated form is dismantled after this exploration, from which a synthetic form is drawn. This synthetic form will then be placed, with its energy, into the psychic system's short-term memory, which is made up of the set of memorized forms of the previously formed representations;

6) depending on the intensity of the characteristics of the apprehended representation, the synthetic form will take its place in short-term memory in a form that is not (with some exceptions) the complete form of the representation. It will be pursued, amplified and specialized, or it will tend to completely fade from the mental landscape, and a new aim will be released with, potentially, the generation of another mental landscape to generate another representation. In all cases, depending on the state of the mental landscape and the current aim, the process of successive steps for generating the "context of the mental landscape, incitation, pre-representation, constructed and experienced representation" starts again by placing a synthesis of the representation with the character-istics of its surrounding mental landscape into organizational memory.

To actually execute this process, it is therefore necessary to precisely define the controllers that will drive the activations and organizational actions of the aggregates:

1) There is a **large organization of regulators** that control and activate the semantic and sensitive conformations of each representation under construction according to its domain, its theme and its characteristics:

i) there are regulators that remove the current context and that generate the current mental landscape by activating and coordinating the other organizational regulators;

ii) there are regulators that will initiate an aim, an incitation, a focus on a precise or a relatively vague theme and others that will generate the pre-representation in the current context by calling the aggregates in organizational memory;

iii) there are regulators that drive the activation and action of the aggregates that make up the explicit representation from the pre-representation, depending on the context provided by the landscape and the incitation of the aim.

2) All of these regulators communicate; they are not independent, nor do they form distinct layers, but they constitute an organization with interactive levels. This co-activation will allow for a very flexible, keen and powerful rational operation.

3) All of these regulators, primarily the regulators driving the deployment of the aggregates, will produce the characteristics of the feeling of apprehension of the representation, according to their intensities and their capacities for influence. There are activations of the regulators of feeling, intention, interrogation, naming, characterization, openness or closure and there are obviously regulators insuring coherence of all the local aspects of the representation under construction so that it will be globally well–organized and homogeneous.

4) Such a psychic system is therefore interpreted and understood as a complex dynamic system that controls itself in order to construct conformations, which is fundamentally a system for controlling the forms that it constructs to apprehend them and to memorize them synthetically.

Therefore, the role and the characteristics of the regulators that lead to the construction of the mental representation and its apprehension are major. They are components that act at several levels as local organizational fields, which activate the components of memory to construct conformations of aggregates. This type of system resembles the autopoetic systems of Morin [MOR 14a].

All of these regulators must coactivate continuously to regulate their actions. Such a system is extremely efficient, but it is rather fragile, especially because of the action of the attractors. The failure of certain regulators that begin to operate rigidly and systematically without coactivating with others, or the action of the attractors, will be the cause of many mental pathologies.

1.11. Unification between regulators and neuronal aggregates: the morphological model of the generating forms

What we have so far defined explains that the control components provoke the operation, stabilities and instabilities in the system. For this purpose, the system uses the notion of control over a set of neuronal aggregates that itself supports the components with semantic characteristics and whose organized union will generate the meaning of the emergent representation. We are taking an approach that distinguishes semantic components from their control, but that does not specify precisely enough which components carry the semantics or how they are formed. However, we have a neuronal system in which neurons are strongly connected by the synapses; everything is neuronal and connected, and we therefore must further specify the notion of memory and action in such a system. And we assert that this memory is not an accumulation of already formed components that can be extracted and activated, as in computer memory, but that there are constructive components that reconstruct the forms of what was memorized in order to be able to use it dynamically.

We therefore assert that all of the components that organize themselves to produce representations, that provide semantics and that exercise control are components that have geometric forms, allowing for their aggregation and that are made up of spatialized aggregates of neurons. We are going to redefine the general meaningful components of the neuronal system at the level of the formation of representations, which will be spatial forms made up of groups of highly coactive neurons. And there will be two kinds of such forms in the geometry of the neuronal system: those that exercise morphological control and those that form geometrically to represent the components of memory. We will call these components **generating forms**.

Generating forms

We assert that components intervening functionally at the level of the generation of mental representations are of one single category: they are geometric and energetic components configured in the neuronal network that have their own proactive capability that pushes them to co-activation, that deploy semantic characteristics or control characteristics that their activity will express through influence on and association with other components. We will call them **generating forms**, and they are materially and spatially of two types: **generating forms for memory** and **generating forms for regulation**. The forms for memory anchor the components of organizational memory, and the forms for regulation ensure the control for all levels in the system. These components make up a dynamic self-organization; the entire system will be, at several levels, made up of components with geometric aspects that conform to each other, activate each other and co-activate in organizational cooperation to engender, through their actions, the emergence of a representation that will be apprehended and perceived for a brief instant. These forms have a property that distinguishes them from permanent mathematical functions: their activation always brings about their structural and organizational modification because they memorize the activities of the system so that they exist continuously for the duration.

The problem will therefore be to define the extent of the activities of these generating forms for exercising semantic and control actions, which will determine the characteristics of emergent generations and the psychological profile of the generator of these emergences. The generating forms are therefore well-structured groups of neurons connected by the actions of the synapses, which allows them to have geometric forms that are similar to flat or twisted linear wires, to flat or curved layers, to coiling or enveloping forms, or to toruses or polyhedrons. The distribution of active neurons in these generating forms will represent their characteristics, which will allow, for example, the representation of words in a language and the formation of sentences through dynamic geometric aggregations. These components have a geometry that represents both their semantics and their capacity for connective action through the propagation of energy toward other forms. These components are made to act through connectivity and to form aggregates of active generating forms producing representations. In the brain, they will be situated in specific domains representing the system's instances and the subdomains of these instances, allowing them to specify their semantic characteristics and their roles in specific actions.

As asserted, there are two kinds of generating forms. There is the regulatory kind, which corresponds to the regulators we have defined (the forms for regulation), which will determine the tendencies of the system such as needs, desires, the need to produce an aim, the need to generate a representation and the need to memorize every representation, which will produce the feeling of thinking. These forms are active morphological graphs formed of connections between small clusters of neurons. And then there will be the forms of memory, which will represent components of organizational memory at every level and will be formed of small active networks of clearly localized neurons. Things that are memorized by the psychic system are not components that are constructed and located in an immense memory that should be searched for and activated through localization; rather they are components that are reconstructed each time, starting from an incitement of the components made for this reconstruction. Organizational memory is dynamic and constructive, with a conformation deploying the categories of components apt to produce specific characteristics through hierarchies of subdomains and has nothing to do with computing-type memory or with a dictionary in which the memorized facts are categorized. We will develop the way in which the reconstructions of memory are formed.

There are thus two kinds of generating forms in the psychic system when it forms that are operational as soon as the infant's brain is conceived and active. At this stage, the generating forms will apprehend the developing body and the information coming from the senses and will generate very simple representations. The system will systematically become more complex, continuously, notably when the brain grows in size, and will then become more complex through use. At the level of the functional individual, the brain is made up of generating forms that characterize all of its categories of idea production. We can assert that it is organized by the generating forms of regulations, which will produce all of the new forms of the system during a continuous learning process. The forms of initial regulation will be able to make the system more complex because it is not a cluster of neurons that functions mechanically but an evolving organization of conformations that continuously generates representations. There will therefore be basic generating forms of regulation that will determine fundamental characteristics and that will form the beginning of the psychic system, with layers of aggregates shaped and spatialized to produce emergences of representations. Then there will be the operation of this dynamic complex system: the use of forms, the modification of certain generating forms and the continuous creation of new forms, especially memory forms.

The notion of a mental landscape is now very clear. It is the organized set of active generating forms that make up a geometric organization of several active networks having specific characteristics, and these geometric characteristics will indicate the semantic and emotional characteristics of the psychic system at that time.

The groups of active aggregates that we can see using neuronal imaging are sets of neurons in generating forms. The aggregate is only a local and one-time image of a group of neurons; this group is a component of an organization whose spatiality can represent conceptual components, like the words in a sentence or memorized images, and that is in contact spatially with other aggregates in other generating forms. The geometric and informational characteristics of each generating form provide its type, its meaning, its role and its importance. Its action at the physical level is an energetic wrapping that organizes the connections between these groups of neurons and engages in informational coactivity with other neuronal groups located in other connected generating forms. The entire psychic structure must therefore be considered in regards to the following three characteristics, which should be considered in this order: the geometric aspects, the informational characteristics and the deployed and propagated energetic intensity. The knowledge of these forms is an excellent research domain for inquiry.

Every use of a generating form in the production of a representation entails the communicational activity of these neuronal aggregates and coactivity with other forms that are connected to its structure to a variable degree. And the act of producing the representation amounts to constructing a conformation made up of several forms whose parts are very active and also strongly coactive. This distinguishable part of very active forms is differentiated from the rest of the system by the process of evaluation and by proceeding with the structural and organizational modification of each form, if the equivalences that led to its aggregative activity are new, through new links between aggregates or new flows of energy between some aggregates. The system's memory exists in its very organization, and that is why we call it organizational memory, and it is modified, reinforced, or altered to a variable degree, depending on the intensity of the organization of each representation that is generated.

The activated generating forms of memory will be modified to a variable degree with each use. They are initially activated by generating small generating forms that coactivate, regroup and unify. These regroupings and this structured unification, which produces the new representations, will potentially change the roles of the forms that constitute it. Certain forms may have been able to be introduced into the representation by augmenting the characteristics and the system through the action of the generating forms of regulation that will analyze the representation and will then modify the coactive connections between the aggregates of the forms of memory that constitute the new landscape. Thus, the memory will modify itself by keeping itself up-to-date. This memory therefore has two characteristics of the active components of the generating form for memory, one representing symbolic characteristics and another representing the connections with other forms of memory.

The construction of the generating forms of memory occurs as follows:

1) a generating form of regulation is active, and its activity compels it to initiate the forms of memory. It therefore contains in itself the activators of the forms of memory and will choose to initiate a form of memory;

2) it activates a certain number of neuronal groups in its context that will make up the components of memory of the activated form;

3) it compels these neurons to activate according to a geometric form that will be the expression of the thing in memory to be activated;

4) the groups of neurons coactivate and form their networks of synaptic connections so that the dynamic graph of their relationships has the conformation of a precise kind, representing the memorized thing that is then active;

5) if this generating form of regulation must compel other forms of memory, it does so, and it compels coactive connections between all these forms of memory by delivering energy and information through its synaptic connections;

6) it therefore consists of a conformation of memory that is localized in the mental landscape and that is the representation being generated;

7) meanwhile, other generating forms of regulation have completed the same thing at the same time. These generating forms will communicate to aggregate, unify and command the sets of forms of memory in the representation, which then will be stabilized and therefore available;

8) the representation in the mental landscape is available to be analyzed by the generating forms of regulation of the conscious, which will produce perception and cause these characteristics to be memorized.

There is therefore a process for creating constructive memory calls through the act of controlling the forms of regulation. These forms of regulation, which are fundamental components of the system, have structures that enable the following actions:

1) these forms have the well-defined structure of an action network, with a conformation that can be changed but that must maintain a specific structural foundation to prevent itself from becoming deficient or inoperable;

2) they are active if they have been activated by an energy flow; if not, they are dormant, and their structure does not participate in any of the system's activities;

3) they contain, in the form of networks of neurons having specific conformations, instructions about the type of activity that specifies their actions, according to their types, and that are part of the general framework: initiating forms of memory, initiating actions in the sensory system, responding to tangible information from the system and initiating the acts of activation or deactivation of other forms of regulation.

We have seen in the previous sections that certain regulators are always active; as a result, certain forms of regulation that have the same functional type as these regulators will always be active: a form of regulation analyzing the senses and initiating, for this, the creation of forms of memory, a form initiating an aim, a form initiating tendencies, impulses, emotions, etc. The continuous activation of forms of regulations leading to the generation of forms of memory practically drives the persistence of these forms of memory. In the background of the mental landscape, there is a permanent physical image that provides an image of the body and what it perceives.

All of the forms that should be active characterize the psyche, and their characteristics have been very clearly specified by psychiatrists and psychologists, who have defined the importance of certain impulsive forms leading to the definition of types and psychic characteristics.

The creation of new generating forms of regulation is a powerful specialty of this system. There can be a specialization from a generating form of regulation that is frequently used to provide the system with more possibilities to generate emergences of specific representations. When a form of regulation acts frequently by activating specific forms of memory, thereby forming a category of activated facts of memory, a new form of regulation can be generated that is based on the old one, so that it no longer generates this class of facts of memory. It is a regulating subform; it is the formation of a specific type of thoughts, a focus. And it can be created through generalization, thus conceptually surpassing two forms of generating regulation.

There is also the possibility of the generation of a new form of regulation in the frame where the generating forms of regulation make up the current representation, producing a very complicated aspect in the mental landscape with different domains that are not producing general coherence with a unifying emergence, and therefore no clear feeling. If this form has come into being repeatedly, leading to the production of non-coherent emergences that are badly perceived, action will be taken by a trending generating form, a fundamental organizational regulating form that has shaped the system from the beginning and that will tend to create a new generating form based on the characteristics of the forms of memory and the active, antagonistic forms of regulation, so that coherent types of emergences are produced. This is an act of organized coherence in the system that does not use higher reason in any way: it is a question of producing coherent and clearly perceived emergences when the usual generating forms do not manage to do so.

Creation of new generating forms of regulation

Through its operation and its use of the underlying fundamental generating forms of regulation, whose role will allow for coherence increasing complexity of the operation of the system, can become more complex on the control level. With this fundamental activity generating forms of regulation, every generating form of regulation can be brought to create new generating forms of regulation through specializations or generalizations.

In order for a new form of regulation to be created, there have to be very specific conditions and a very specific process that must occur. This is relatively similar to the process of the self-generation of a new structure in computing. We have asserted that the system that produces emergences of representations has an organizational generating form that tends to balance and add complexity to the system. This generating form of regulation is the form that will extend so far as to generate normal, simple and satisfying emergences, and also to resolve the distinctions between antagonistic tendencies and anomalies in emergences. This organizational generating form has nothing to do with the conscious, but it is the form of control that allows the conscious to operate correctly in a permanent way.

It is therefore an evolving psychic system that will create new generating forms as necessary during the individual's physical development, then as necessary because of social adaptation and learning, through the practice of economic, sexual and cultural life. We can therefore assert that the human psychic system is initially an organization with generating forms inherited from its position in the living being, but with very strong potential for creating new generating forms of regulation, which are enabled by its social and cultural life in highly organized and, especially, highly evolving communities.

1.12. The morphological and semantic conformation of the psychic system

We can therefore think of the psychic system as being composed of a large number of components having specific forms that are often intermingled with characteristics of informational, sensitive and semantic actions that are situated in specific domains, such as the localization of psychic instances. The generating forms of regulation are structures of neuronal aggregates that are characterized by their geometric form, their energy and their characteristics of semantic incitement. These are strictly forms with three spatial dimensions, representing active graphs, which are made up of several groups of strongly connected neurons and which convey energy and information. These forms can share spatial areas, as is the case for deployments of regulating forms situated in different domains, acting and generating the current representation. They are more or less important in size and in spatial deployment, which will make up their geometric complexity. There will be enveloping forms, highly connected forms, fairly closed and isolated forms such as ribbons, cones or spheres. The smaller the size, the more they express specific characteristics. The larger they are spatially at the information and energy level, and the more divided they are between different domains, the more they have characteristics of extensive control, which will be the forms of regulation established for specifying the system's fundamental tendencies.

The generating forms of regulation are dormant or active depending on the state of the system's activity, but some will always be active, such as those that apprehend sensory information and the organizational generating form. When they are active, these forms are highly coactive at several levels because they have a spatial characteristic that makes them routinely communicative through the sharing of parts of their layers. Each form can therefore communicate in parallel with several other forms, which allowing for the production of rich and complex representations. In every case, these forms can have and dispense energy to activate, energy that they receive through their action in the substrate of neurons and the system's specific chemical components. According to their geometric configuration, they are made to be able to confront each other or to be relatively indifferent to influence from other forms. The scale of observation of the brain's psychic activity should therefore be carried out based on, firstly, the classification and then the identification of the activity of all of these forms.

The generating forms of regulation carry meaning and are considered as localized in the psychic system's four general instances – the unconscious, the center of emotions, the preconscious and the conscious – and, in fact, they create the existence of these four instances through their roles. The fifth instance, defined as the systemic layer and which houses important regulators, also exists in this model. This is where the tendency for general organizational regulation exists, which connects all of the generating forms at the informational level, regulates the organization and leads to the existence of the general space of regulation and of the semantic morphology of the coactive regulating forms that is the psychic system on its neuronal substrate.

The system is then seen as a machine under continuous self-organization in three-dimensional space that never stops activating and reconstructing the sets of neuronal aggregates situated in specific spatial conformations of the generating forms of memory by producing deformations, reshapings, separations and reunions; all of the activities that have algebraic characteristics also have particularly geometric characteristics as well as obvious semantic characteristics. The notion of geometric conformation therefore becomes central. There are active geometric forms that represent meaningful components in the generated representation. But these forms are coactive and will organize among themselves. Thus, there are forms that will append themselves to others, which will embed themselves in others, which will surround others. Through these multiple geometric actions, the system can organize countless conformations that produce apprehended mental representations. We can see the internal representations of spoken or heard sentences; these sentences have forms with multiple conformations that make them rich. There will also be generating forms of regulation that are often very active, and through these it will be possible to characterize the individual's general psychic type.

Such unification between neuronal aggregates and generating forms of regulation clearly expresses the central role of control in the generation of ideas, a role that must obviously be clearly specified through the semantic characteristics carried by the activated components expressing the meaningful characteristics of the representations.

We can define the **main characteristics of a generating form of regulation** in the system:

– its domain in the different instances and specific parts of the brain;

– its geometric characteristics and its geometric category;

– its scope, its internal graph of communications between neuronal groups, with its importance in nodes and arcs, as well as its spatial deployment;

– the energy it should have available in order to activate;

– its specific semantic characteristics, its ontological class;

– its expressive role and its types of possible actions;

– its actions and its programs for constructing conformations for generating forms of memory in groups of neurons, which is very explicit for linguistic forms;

– its history and its evolution;

– its positive acquaintances: the other generating forms of regulation to which it is connected for cooperation;

– its negative acquaintances: the other generating forms with which it is opposed during its activity;

– its ability for memorization, deformation, development and change in volume;

– the frequency of its activation and the specification of its importance;

– its domination over other generating forms of regulation, its neutrality or its subordinate characteristic/s.

The **main characteristics of a generating form of memory** are as follows:

– the generating forms of regulation that are its generator;

– the information and the program that the group of neurons must receive to activate and adapt in order to serve through its configuration;

– its spatial conformation and its geometric openness or closure;

– its type and therefore its local importance;

– its action of calling the necessary forms or the calling for their generation to amplify the process of its activity;

– its capacity for consistency or evolution: its stability;

And the operation of the system with the generating forms must therefore be as follows:

1) there are active generating forms of regulation, including those that ensure the interpretation of sensory information coming from the body and the generation of the aim; the brain is never without activity,

and there is an active mental landscape that is specific or vague depending on the system's state of attention;

2) the generating forms of regulation that have the role of initiating an aim to activate and regulate themselves, and an aim is activated in the mental landscape. If the aim is weak, the current mental landscape is used (state with limited attention);

3) generating forms of regulation relative to the domain of the aim are concurrently activated; they regulate themselves, and some will be sufficiently active to form a coherent and coactive set;

4) the conformation with the influential active forms of regulation that were inactive and that may possibly complete them, enriching them through geometric and energetic operations and activating the generating forms of memory;

5) the general organization of the forms of regulation and the forms of memory is constituted and stabilized, its components no longer activate others; they form a relatively geometrically stable conformation. The form of representation in the mental landscape is therefore able to be perceived;

6) the generating forms of regulation, which have the role of validating the available conformation made up of forms of memory and regulation to operate. They evaluate the conformations of the representation by detaching syntheses. Here, the system of generating forms that causes the feeling of thinking globally evaluates, through domains and components, the conformations that have been created as conformations. This action targets memorization before any change in these conformations in the landscape in order to initiate another landscape. This action requires analysis and the expenditure of force and energy by the generating forms to realize the modification of the conformations. This action is an internal sensation that has all of the characteristics of a physical sensation with action: this is the feeling of thinking about something that is being produced;

7) having perceived the representation, the system accomplishes its required memorization by passing it through short-term memory with local memorization of the connections between the constituents of the

components; the meta-regulator for continuous operation dampens the current aim, which is no longer dominant;

8) the generating forms of regulation that initiate aims reactivate in order to define a new one, and the process of thought generation initiates a new generating action.

This process is clearly described in an algorithmic way, because it is composed of a succession of events in space and time, with certain actions realized in parallel. A question can be raised concerning the generating forms of regulation activated by the aim: what are the chosen forms and how strong is the coherence of the control components for generating a conformation that is clearly coherent with the aim and that fully uses organizational memory? This question concerns the coherence and the strength of the psychic system, and it will be necessary to specify the action of control of the generating forms that permit the production of emergences.

1.13. The processing component of the visual sense with generating forms

The use of the senses allows for positioning in the surrounding reality, by giving the body the ability to behave and to act effectively by means of the generation of specific representations. The information provided by the senses is analyzed and processed in fairly complex ways, such as with vision, which allows for the representation of a series of images of reality that are not only three dimensional but are made up of things that are perceived according to their relative positions, their colors and their actions, as well as their local and predictable trajectories for objects in motion. The senses continuously generate mental constructions that, based on each target of observation, can be highly developed by the forms of regulation.

A view of surrounding reality is a construct that is highly developed because it provides the positions and the three-dimensional forms of objects as well as information about the size of these objects through comparative scales and relative distances, and it enables a focus on zones or on specific objects to apprehend their characteristics, all while remaining in the domain of the real global landscape. For this, based on the visual apprehension that is initially a request for representation of its position in space–time, the system constructs the sequence of visual representations by requesting focus on parts, components and details of components. All vision is therefore a regular sequence of representations; it is a flow of mental constructs according to the requests of aims concerning deepenings, comparisons and distinctive features. It is absolutely not a complete picture that is initially grasped and then processed, as is the case with traditional image analysis in computing that begins with tables of pixels; rather, it is a series of constructs that are produced by requesting that the gaze focus on certain apprehended parts that the system of representation wants to apprehend in detail. Therefore, in this continuous representational process, the memory is strongly activated, and the constructed representations take knowledge about familiar images into account. There are things considered as familiar and common that are clearly identified, and there are things that are barely or not at all familiar, whose characteristics will have to be specified so that they can be identified. The process focuses on the thing to be specified, because the order to focus on the eyes operates implicitly, thereby developing the cognitive characteristic in the apprehension of the image.

Here, it is very clear that internal visual representation uses categories of mental landscapes corresponding to common situations and to the things that are usually observed. We can assert that many categories and families of mental landscapes of vision exist, according to one's habits. In what is apprehended, the geometric forms represented by the internal generating forms absolutely do not correspond exactly to the geometric forms of the real things that are seen; rather, they are an organization of conformations of generating forms with characteristics of geometric description and relationships that endlessly adapt to apprehended reality, depending on the focus. But how are these internal generating forms constituted, and how do they function to represent the seen landscape? This is the problem that will be resolved by explicating the relationships between the real observed landscape and the mental landscape that will represent it.

A real landscape is a domain of space containing multiple volumetric components that create its structure and its organization. It is apprehended by the vision, grasped as structurally comprehensible and knowable in relation to the observer's internal circumstances when seeing the real landscape. The observer constructs what is commonly called a cognitive map, which is a sort of Euclidean space where the evaluated distances can be summed up and therefore provide every distance between one point and another to complete a trip. Apprehending real landscapes always entails a certain understanding through visual habit; there is no radical objectivity, but the interpretation is sometimes very sophisticated. There is a relationship of tangible apprehension between a human being and the environment where the human finds themselves; the view of real things is not an objective image of physical characteristics, but rather an understanding that is both sensitive, geometric and cognitive, and that will be interpreted by the conscious. A visual aim leads to a focus on one or more domains that will necessarily have semantic characteristics supplied by memory.

There are generating forms that will lead to the formation of the representation of what is seen, and there are generating forms that will be three-dimensional interpretations of things in the real landscape that will organize to form a correspondence with observed reality. There are therefore numerous generating forms that will be activated and that will represent the components of reality. We can therefore assert that there are numerous **generating forms of regulation and of visual memory**.

The mental form of an apprehended view

The mental form of a seen thing that is presented in the mental landscape to be apprehended consciously is twofold: it is initiated by visual generating forms that lead to a type of visual and observational input with geometric and three-dimensional Euclidean characteristics, and with visual generating forms that represent the constructs of the components that are visually apprehended. Then, there are generating forms that cognitively and sensitively interpret the visual generating forms, which are cognitive components with semantic classifications of these components and which are usually generating forms of a linguistic and therefore conceptual type. There is thus an automatic preinterpretation of what is seen in order to adapt the structure of the representation in the mental landscape, and then there is the apprehension of the conformation of this generating representation, which will be both sensitive and cognitive.

There will therefore be types of generating forms of regulation that will initiate the local activity of visual generating forms in order to communicate with cognitive-type generating forms of regulation so that these forms, in cooperation, generate the associated and corresponding designations. It is therefore the question of a complex operation that associates the characteristics of reality with the concept than we have of it, and that will determine our knowledge of the world, where part of the designation, as well as acquired knowledge, is associated with everything that is apprehended by the senses.

Observing a landscape therefore consists of interpreting a sequence of conformations of mental representations and grasping some of these objects in order to name and interpret them in a continuous manner. Seeing is an act of interpretation that orders the eyes to focus on certain components so that they furnish internal conformations that are immediately interpreted as familiar or unfamiliar objects, that are identified, and categorized and that produce feelings that modify the current mental landscape, where the generation of interpretations continues. The external forms that hold the focus produce the conformations of internal forms in the mental landscape along with a contextual domain that is the interpretation of the set of the regarded real landscape, which is always available in the background through general forms. We therefore have an internal mental landscape that has a precise local relationship with the external real landscape, and which will lead, through inevitable abstraction in the operation of the psyche, to its understanding, by providing it with semantic characteristics using the knowledge of names and by producing geometric estimates. And what is apprehended is an interpretation of reality, with those things selected through focus because they were recognized, parts of the noticed things, connections between things, the actions of things, comparative dimensions.

The relationship between reality and internal forms is not at all a geometric isomorphism; there is no mathematic similarity between the real landscape and the internal conformations. There are visual generating forms with neuronal aggregates making explicit the structures, colors and textures of components seen by the eyes that are positioned to respect distances, separations and domains, and there is a systematic, elementary interpretation of these components, as well as a cognitive and sensitive interpretation of these internal representatives. There is an immediate accumulation of conformations expressing recognition of the sensation associated with familiar things, and it is this general conformation in the visual mental landscape that will be apprehended as perceived consciousness. This is the mental landscape proposed to the conscious, representing components with two meanings: internal images of real objects and their usual meanings, their cognitive categories and the feelings that they inspire. With this duality, there will be, in the apprehension of the representation, the knowledge and feeling provided by these components of the observed landscape, which lead to a pursuit of the investigation of a newly focal point, or the passage to apprehension of another identified thing in the mental landscape that exists in the real landscape. And it is precisely for this reason that things that are unusual and unfamiliar are immediately noticed, because they have no associated meaningful connotation and are an anomaly in the set of forms with these two meanings.

The apprehension of the visual generating form will grasp things, their conformations, their denotations and their tangible appraisals. This will entail a deepening of certain components and the disposition of certain others as subordinate. The mental landscape will remain in its general form, but the mental apprehension will order a focus on certain components to apprehend other characteristics. Short-term memory will retain the global form, and certain focuses will be more tangible. Here, the psychic system demonstrates a form of deployment in a domain that systematically makes use of the organizational memory.

The generating forms representing components in the surrounding space are therefore components that define two characteristics, one expressing the physical aspects of components apprehended by the vision and the other expressing semantic and tangible aspects of these components. These new conformations are constructed with a focus on what is contextual to what is actually focused on, but which remains geometrically well positioned in relation to what was previously focused on, and can therefore be apprehended by scanning the real landscape. We should consider that each geometrically apprehended form deploys its meaning through those characteristics of its physical texture, with its volume specifying it in its context, its apparent structural complexity, its color and its common or novel characteristics. For this, there are elementary geometrical forms in memory that define the geometric types of fundamental components, such as broken lines and their horizontal, vertical or diagonal placement, rectangles, circles and all distortions of these components, which lose their regularity but maintain their relationships with these fundamental types.

This calls into question research concerning the development of systems of artificial recognition based on clouds of pixels captured by cameras and stored in matrices that are then analyzed section by section during processing by semantic interpreters that will try to recognize the components: the semantics must be done simultaneously with image capture, and object recognition must lead to a control of the continuous focus of the visual apparatus, which must therefore be multiple and not unitary, and produce a simple layer of pixels in order to construct a series of representations intentionally constructed by a system of apprehension.

Vision is a very important behavioral action in the psychic system for the positioning of the individual; it is a continuous action, sometimes underlying other superficial representations, which allows for other more profound representations. The process of apprehending the representation that we have defined, which causes conscious awareness of what is given to be apprehended and maintains the interpretations of seen things in short-term memory, operates centrally here. The usual vision of the environment is a major process that, depending on experience and with a well-evaluated understanding of things, situates living beings in their environments by being specific to different species depending on their physical aptitudes and their lifestyles. This visual cognitive apprehension applies to all species that have a visual center: every animal that sees apprehends, according to its way of life and its acquired habits, the meaning of what they see as being familiar and congruent or novel and to be avoided, or to be considered more carefully, to be apprehended as interesting.

1.14. The decisive intention to think

We can now address the major problem of making the decision to think, taking into account the well-structured aspect of what will be proposed to the conscious when it apprehends what is seen so that it perceives, appreciates, analyzes and generates aims. The conscious is not a meta-controller above a system that simply generates specific idea emergences; it is a constructor of generating forms that apprehends and synthetically memorizes; it is a constructor that operates organizationally with all of the impulsive, cognitive and sensitive controllers at all levels. So, what is the extent of the mastery of the conscious in the production of ideas? This is the central question concerning the operation of the psychic system: how does the conscious master the development of its idea productions, how does it use its organizational memory intentionally, how do the generating forms that come from the tendencies and the impulses take their place implicitly and what directly uses organizational memory by bringing forms to take place in the emergences of the representations?

The problem of the mastery of the conscious

In the mental landscape where the effects of vision are produced, the psychic system generates pre-representations with aspects that are both cognitive and sensitive and that have used organizational memory. These forms are deployed and enriched by generating forms in the conscious, and then apprehended and perceived in the conscious through investigation and synthetic construction. So, what is the mastery of consciousness in the produced thoughts that are based on voluntary aims, and how does it construct, through its control, representations that are mastered by the aims?

We will respond in a constructivist manner to this question. A generating form that is able to define and impose a choice of aim in a carefully defined context must exist, and this controller must not be subordinate to generating forms of regulation that impose affective aspects, specific forms of memory, or trending aspects, nor to generating forms of the attractor type that impose specific qualifications on each representation by altering the aims. It is therefore necessary to assert that a generating form exists that imposes mastery over the choice of an aim in all mental landscapes.

Such a generating form does actually exist: it is the fundamental generating form of regulation that expresses the will to think. We will call this form the **generating form for decision-making intention**. This form exists in the conscious and the systemic layer; it is always active and available, waiting for activity, asking itself to produce an action that defines the characteristics of an aim. It will be necessary for the process of producing representations with the defined aim. But the problem is to always be able to use it, to not be in a constrained situation where tendencies impose aims or alter choices made about the proposed aim.

Generating form for decision-making intention

There exists a fundamental generating form of regulation at the meta level that waits for the choice of an aim exercised by the generating form of the generation of an aim to produce a thought in the context of the mental landscape in order to be able to proceed to a series of coherent thoughts on a chosen theme. It is the **generating form for intentional decision making**, which will produce the choice of aim in the context of the mental landscape where a number of regulating forms are active, and which initiates the regulating action to generate the representation according to the theme proposed by the aim. This is the internal continuous action that each individual must do in the active psychic system, so that this form waiting for the aim will be provided and will produce the series of wanted representations. This generating form of meta regulation, which is always waiting for an intention when no precise aim has been initiated, is the dominant generating form, but it is not the only one that is meta, and, to make it more effective when one wants the decision to think to be activated, a certain mastery of the physical, sensitive and psychological state is required.

The generating forms on the meta level are all situated in a specific domain of the conscious and there are always several to be activated. There is the one that imposes the choice of an aim, those providing the generating characteristics of the mental landscape through calls to active facts in memory, and those activating the perceptible representations coming from the body in action, of which the vision apprehends the environment in order to be able to behave in it. It is therefore necessary to be able to provide the decision to act to the form that generates the choice of the aim in the context of the mental landscape, which must be open. This is typically, habitually done with a regular practice of self-mastery. Providing meaning to a generating form at the meta level is the result of its regular activation, which gives it supremacy compared to the others.

The important fact, and the one that must always occur according to the form of the intentional decision, is to choose an aim and to engage the conscious to use it to produce a first representation. Moreover, the aim is taken from the mental landscape. The mental landscape is always very rich; it contains active generating forms of memory coming from the preceding representations and from their contexts; it contains forms expressing the current sensation; and it contains a physical representation, all of whose parts are available. It is therefore sufficient to use the generating form of the choice of aim so that the generating form for decision-making intention asks to request and to set a theme from those available in the mental landscape. The chosen theme will then be the aim, the generation of a pre-representation, and a first representation. Then, there will be the deepening and production of a series, often short, of representations that form a surge by soliciting more specific aims and by acceding to generating forms of the organizational memory.

The psychic system therefore possesses a meta subsystem that leads it to intentionally and continuously produce representations when it is active. These representations can be truly deliberate through the incitement of the production of an aim that the form of the decision-making intention engages, which is an apprehension of this generating form about itself that the psychic system provides for itself. This aptitude for wanting to produce thoughts signifies that the psychic system has a reflexive, self-organizing function at this level that is waiting to activate a commitment for this generating form of this meta regulation. This generating form of intentional decision-making, which produces the aim, therefore defines the idea of consciousness and of will in the system. We can say that the psychic system waits for a request to be given to this meta generating form, which can allow it to be activated by defining an aim in the context of the mental landscape, and which, if not, will provide the supremacy to another generating form of the aim connected to the context and to the affectivity, with vague and simply sensitive representations.

The intentional consciousness of the system

> The generating form of meta regulation for decision-making intention provides self-awareness to the system, in the sense that it engages the production of an internal process of the choice of an aim in the context formed by the mental landscape. It is always active, waiting precisely for the solicitation of an aim, which it enables by providing the mental landscape and organizational memory. The human therefore has a system of consciousness that is constantly waiting for the solicitation of this meta-form. It produces the fact of **wanting to think** and categorizes the organizational reflexivity of the psychic system, which can produce the wanted representations in itself and for itself, and which otherwise produces opportune representations calling the sensations according to the context or the simple activity of memory. It supervises the active facts of memory in the mental landscape and the active facts in organizational memory in order to use it.

This fundamental generating form is therefore active with associated generating forms, allowing for the choice, in organizational memory or in the affective domain of the current mental landscape, of an instructional theme that will be the new aim with a new mental landscape to form the new series of representations. It is the representative of the autonomy of the psychic system, which produces intentional mental representations on its own and for itself. It waits for the human, in an active state in its conscious system, to furnish the internal forms of thought by concentrating on notions and ideal instructions. These instructions will constitute the theme of the aim and will deploy it immediately in representation. We are clearly describing an internal local process where the consciousness of the psychic system has an active position in relation to itself, allowing it to specify available instructions in its internal language, and it will be able to make itself deploy representations that will be experienced through analysis and synthetic memorization. The internal language used to indicate the aim's theme, which will initiate the process of generation of the new representation, is obviously not made up of simple generational forms that are linguistic or sensitive, but operates in a mental landscape driven by the generating forms of regulation, which express tendencies, impulses, needs and especially access to organizational memory.

The use of the generating form for the production of aims on a conceptual and deep theme signifies a detachment from all significant contextual effect, of all invasive sensitive apprehension, of all imperative surges from memory. A certain learning process uses this generating form when the attention for the generation of the series of aims moves toward very intentional and deep use, and it must be placed into a good context, allowing for its wide use. If not, it is easy to allow thoughts to be produced without real will, by using reality and the facts of memory and by allowing the flow of thoughts generated without specific intention to be experienced. This is daydreaming. Furthermore, in social relationships or work, society does not always implement this potential for producing mastery over thought, which demands detachment and concentration. Each must learn for themselves to master their thoughts, in fact to think about the arrival of their thoughts, to evaluate them in a regular fashion, and to focus on deep reasonings, which are always criticized by the self.

1.15. Linguistic capacity in the human conscious

The specific linguistic property of the human being consists of the ability to speak, read and write. It uses cognitive linguistic instructions in most of its mental representations. These are the objects of the real world where reality comes from our world; our organized world that we all share and that allows us to make statements about things and values, to ask questions and to refer to our thoughts in order to evaluate and use them. Language is a means of communication and reflexive investigation, which can refer to itself in speech acts by generating questions. The act of thinking by using language necessarily introduces the notion of the Ego, knowing that we can think what one has thought. Thinking involves the generation of a form of representation, and thinking this thought is the apprehension of the fact that we have produced this thought in its mental form in our psychic system. Here, we can assert the notion of "Ego", which is a profound concept, but which is also a word in our language. And we can assert that "language and consciousness make the world" [WOL 97], that is to say, all apprehension of things is and can remain in language and consciousness, since apprehension of the world is dependent on language as practiced, with cultural research making it possible to surpass this limitation. Thus, Wolf defines three fundamental ontologies for things that include all things that are permanent, as well as events that encompass everything that happens to things, and finally individuals, that is to say those who generate events. It also specifies that language enables the structuring of the world by continuously using these three ontologies: nouns designating things, verbs designating events and pronouns designating people. Can we think "I am thinking about myself" without knowing language and those three meaningful words – noun, verb and personal pronoun – that identify that the question designating one's Ego?

We must try to discover by what property of the psychic system, as modeled in a constructivist fashion, the human manages to discover and use languages represented by utterances and especially by writing that represents sentences, which leads to radical differentiation from all of the other living beings at the level of the use of reflexive memories and conceptual structures in relation to all of the understandable things in reality. Moreover, the question of the use of language cannot avoid addressing the problem of the value of the interpretations of real things, which was clearly posed by Nietzsche a long time ago [NIE 74].

In humans that are awake, there is a permanent tendency to conceive of representations in the psychic system which awaits it with the generation of a desire for expression. It is the expression of the general life impulse that is exercised in its psychic system. There is a very specific and particular process in the human, which initiates the pursuit of the representation of a thing that it has apprehended in most contexts where it apprehends and appreciates characteristics of this thing in the form of depeenings through symbolic identifiers. There is a displacement of the initial desire for apprehension of its sensitive and emotional framework of knowledge so that it continues in a symbolic and cognitive framework. There is thus an engagement with other humans, a desire to produce social acts, to socialize and to cooperate, and a desire to question the other with sentences and to communicate symbolically with them. This is the distinction with other living things.

Language is a social human reality that is completely constructed through the social practices of humans. It has a very deep cultural aspect, but there is also an internal aspect of very important conformations in the psychic system of each human. The origin of language lies in the aptitude of the human psychic system to engender manipulable abstractions that can be communicated by oral or written informational signs, by using them in a collective fashion to create language in a continuous process of use and creation. It is therefore a question of clearly understanding this aptitude and seeing how it is produced in the psychic system and how it becomes the means to make civilizations exist in social reality.

The tendency to internal abstraction

In humans, there is a fundamental tendency to produce representations with abstract symbolic forms, using generating forms that manipulate abstract concepts represented by conformations that embody words that can be very easily combined with each other to form sentences that hold meaning. This is an internal activity of the psychic system where generating forms designate and represent abstract characteristics in linguistic form in relation to the components and the events of reality and can operate on themselves through operations that are regulated by specific generating forms. There are symbolic signifiers and operations on them to connect them, to use them profoundly in groups and to develop them by augmenting their meanings through the formation of new abstract concepts. There will even be operations on the operations of linguistic manipulations with explicit growth, which is typical of the organization of the psychic system. And there will be a symbolization of time and space, which will enable the creation of an internal domain where very powerful conceptual operations will allow for shared knowledge and the cultivation of the world. Many of these internal forms have been learned in cultures, where they have been interpreted, manipulated and developed continuously by being in each person's organizational memory and in the reality of the communicating world.

In the psychic system, there are therefore generating forms whose specific action is to generate abstractions, strictly internal forms that allow the system to operate on itself without necessarily referring to the senses, to the vision or to hearing. There is a large number of generating forms that provide the notion of time and space that are available and that are specified by learned cultural and scientific linguistic forms.

The psychic system is not content to manipulate forms representing images of the things that are seen, heard or smelled; it also manipulates internal forms that are abstract and that define the results of operations of naming and set theory that specify evaluations and that denote signifiers such as words that are able to be associated with other words without designating a specific object in reality. This is the case for a number of verbs such as "to conceive, to extrapolate, to generalize, to extract, etc.", or of nouns such as "infinite, void, emptiness, etc.". We can therefore assert that there are generating forms for abstractions that operate in the instance representing the system's systemic layer, between the conscious and the organizational memory and through the auditory or visual senses, to learn words and their meanings and to learn to formulate sentences that use words by functioning socially through learning and practice. These are therefore generating forms of regulation that operate to coordinate the management of all of the instances of the psychic system. Here, it is a question of a completed form of organizational regulation of a psychic system that is equipped with a very strong organizational capability, and using numerous kinds of set-theoretic and algebraic operations.

In the brain, there will therefore be a specific domain for language where the generating forms of regulation will initiate the production of abstractions and will use specific generating forms of word use. These forms of regulation will activate themselves like set-theoretic and algebraic operators by adapting geometric components in spatialized compositions. These generating forms of abstraction will operate as functions for sentence construction by mixing with themselves, according to the distinctive learned and therefore specific conformations of the different forms of linguistic generators, by using classes of sentences that use verbs, nouns and personal pronouns linked to qualifiers, and these forms will be morphological representations. An uttered or heard sentence will correspond internally to the morphology of the sentence, which can be manipulated at different levels depending on the intensity of its geometric and energetic characteristics, which express semantic intensity.

We therefore assert that, in organizational memory, there are generating forms of linguistic regulation that memorize abstract symbols and fundamental forms to represent words and that produce the operations that enable the representation of different kinds of sentences. We can assert that these linguistic generating forms are categorized according to verbs, nouns, adjectives and other parts of speech by presenting specific morphological characteristics for each part. Therefore, there is a morphological type for verbs and there are additional characteristics that define each of them, which makes a very important constructive categorization in organizational memory; furthermore, the same thing exists for nouns and qualifying adjectives. There are also standard forms for all of the common sentences. And there is more, because there are relationships of proximity between words that one often uses together, verbs associated with nouns and adjectives, and there are obviously well-known sentences that are memorized, which are linguistic generating forms that establish connections between the elementary forms of words. There is therefore a large dynamic network made up of a layer of generating forms that initiate linguistic operations and control multiple subnetworks of words, word–sentences and sentences that activate upon construction, which represents the usable language in the psychic system's organizational memory.

There are also generating forms for initiating the utterance of a sentence used when one wants to utter specific kinds of sentences corresponding to common or novel situations. There will then be classes of mental landscapes corresponding to multiple kinds of sentence utterances, depending on the context of the utterances, which can be explicit or strictly internal when one thinks by using words and sentences. This will characterize the speaker's style.

In thinking, there is the simultaneous activation of a tendency that will activate symbolic constructions, naming with words, and a sensitive tendency that provides impressions and sensitive forms. These two main tendencies are represented by major generating forms of regulation as follows:

1) **the major tendency for sensation**, with connections to impulsive tendencies, which will activate each time a particular desire is expressed while contextual conditions allow it to generate affective representations expressing the emotions, especially pleasure or displeasure;

2) **the major tendency dedicated to abstraction**, which will reify the desire to manipulate internal symbolic forms and with which the individual will be able to continually generate conformations, to find in their organizational memory the objects that satisfy this desire and to manipulate them internally, all while remaining connected to sensation and to things perceived in the environment.

The combination of these two tendencies will form the characteristics in the majority of mental landscapes and will allow for the definition of the majority of the forms of thought. The problem of balance and performance in human beings lies here, in this aptitude to make one of these two tendencies hegemonic, or to not do so. One of these tendencies can be hegemonic, and we must remember that all scientific and philosophical research, as well as all of the positions of deep reflection, are investigations of abstraction before becoming apprehensions for behavior in social life [FOR 16].

By this, we refer to the representation of the concept of abstraction as an internal tendency arising from the ability to consider and to identify objects in the world and the relationships between these objects through the naming of some of their general characteristics, outside of any specific context of sensitive apprehension in which one perceives sensations and emotions, but instead by placing oneself into an internal framework of the conceptual naming of operations about things. This can anchor the very strong notion of human creativity, which is able to conceive of artistic, cultural and scientific objects, before continuing on to their practical fulfillment, which is tangible. It is the transposition of a real object that is apprehended and asserted to exist in the abstract domain of the psychic system as well as in the psychic system in which a domain of abstraction constructed by learning, memorization, manipulation and creativity is featured. The real object is represented by certain traits that characterize and categorize it in a contextual and operational organization. This is the aptitude of a very specific system that we have begun to explicate [CAR 13]. Some living organisms that generate mental representations in their brains, such as monkeys, can symbolize aspects of these representations and appreciate them as such. We can define the specific particularity of humanity in its linguistic aptitude.

Central hypothesis on the linguistic specificity of the human psyche

In the generation of the current representation by the psychic system, the attention is displaced outside of the tangible framework where the senses apprehend specific things to be situated in an internal space created by abstractions represented by forms, where things are represented by dynamic forms that define abstract symbolic components that can be appreciated and manipulated using set-theoretic and algebraic types of operations. This process, which is highly developed in humans and which uses a specific kind of memorization, is the foundation of the linguistic aptitude, which is an activity with very powerful operational capabilities on dynamic symbolic forms. A field of words that can be precisely manipulated by operations to form sentences will be used as a principal generator for most mental representations. In reifying this dynamic space as much as possible by making the central subsystem continuously active, humans have not only distinguished themselves among life forms, but have also created a certain distance from the reality of the world, which apprehends itself tangibly in order to be shared, and this can cause a problem.

The operations used by the psychic system to generate sentences or series of utterances are of a set-theoretic and algebraic type for the very precise structuring of dynamic sets. These are the union, intersection, separation and detachment of a local maximum, the formation of structured networks, subnetworks or hierarchical tree structures, and absorption, evaluation and deformation of a volume or an edge, etc. These operations are done by specific generating forms that are very developed and that produce the linguistic aptitude through their operational functioning. All of these operations are used with precision today by computer scientists, who implement the ability to speak and to respond in autonomous artificial systems. But we must remember that these operations are constructive descriptions and that, in the reality of the psychic system, all constructions lead, more or less, to the modification of the conformation that caused it.

The linguistic ability enables not only the naming and designation of real objects, but also and especially the planning of collective actions, the conception and production of precisely composed components, and then the evaluation of these plans to improve them. All of this is constructive, from thoughts to social structures, allowing for the production of very structured activities for creating innumerable technological creations. But what is there in this linguistic aptitude that enables the understanding of the reality in which we live, the understanding of life and the universe, the understanding of space and time? Here, we are dealing with a deep problem that has been developed by many philosophers, among whom

Nietzsche has clearly formulated the distinction about what in reality and what about reality can be expressed in language by specifying the limit of the linguistic aptitude [NIE 73]. Our constructivist approach to the generation of mental representations in the psychic system, which is absolutely of a material nature that can aggregate dynamic forms under a specific control to produce emergences, leads to a picture of the limits of what can be represented by the production of representations. We will develop this in the section dedicated to implementing an artificial psychic system in a computer.

1.16. An assessment of the functioning of the human psychic system

The model that we have presented of the human psychic system is based on a major question: how can a system made up of many small components that are highly connected generate representational forms at the level of bodily sensation and also represent symbolic assessments of things in the world at multiple levels? To answer this question, we have taken a strictly constructivist approach, the attitude of the computer scientist that models systems to create a completely constructible conception. The computer scientist must first understand the system's performance in its entirety, everything that can be known about it through scientific approaches, and then begin creating their model, representing its functioning at every level, which in the human psychic system is a question of highly novel organizational self-control. Thus, we have developed the notion of generating forms, which expresses symbolism and exercises control.

The human's generating forms, which allow them to create abstractions and to enter into the domain of naming and linguistic manipulations, are highly developed, and they are learned and amplified by the practices of social and cultural life. These generating forms allow for the abstraction of reality in generated representations in order to make many relationships function and thus to name, to class, to categorize, to link concepts and to conceptually connect the relationships between ideas. They allow for the abstraction of sets of abstractions, by going very far into the generating possibilities.

By the concept of abstraction, we clearly mean an aptitude for considering and defining objects in the world via an identity attributed to them by some of their characteristics outside of a specific context of tangible apprehension by placing them into an abstract general framework that makes extensive use of the organizational memory. We therefore propose a hypothesis about human uniqueness.

Hypothesis about human uniqueness

In most of the psychic system's representations, there is a displacement of the attention of one's sensitive framework for perceiving things via the senses into an internal space of abstraction where things are represented by dynamic, manipulable systems that are perceptible as such using all of the operations of organizational memory. This process of interiorization, which makes extensive use of specific memories, is the foundation for linguistic ability, which is an action on dynamic internal symbols in which a highly manipulable field of words and sentences is used as a domain for generating representations of things. By reifying this field as much as possible, human beings create the major distinguishing feature of their species among the living.

We can also say that the human brain is linked to the hands and fingers that form a unified structure with two components. The human uses tools, but a large number of animal species also use tools, including species that swim, fly and live on land. The tool is a common object for a number of animal species [POU 17], but what distinguishes the human relationship to tools is that they use many of them to construct countless, highly organized things that they first see in their mind by conceiving plans for complex compositions in all their details. Their hands, which use and construct, are therefore delicately controlled organs that are strongly tied to the development of abstractions in the psyche.

We propose that this desire for abstraction is a fundamental regulator undertaking the abstraction of apprehended things, but that will always remain linked to the controllers activating the sensory subsystem. The regulators of the sensory subsystem express the body's sensitive impulses toward pleasure through the senses, and they express and unfold according to the context and the current physical state. Very often, the sensitive, impulsive controllers, as well as those that tend toward abstraction, will activate simultaneously, but sometimes, they will activate independently. Here lies the entire problem of the human's complex and ultimately fragile psychology and provides a key for all of the neurotic types of pathologies, which have led societies to create psychologists, psychiatrists, psychoanalysts, sexologists, etc.

So, how have humans, with such powerful psychic systems, been able to construct societies with inequality, confrontations, wars, genocides, massacres and slaughters, and advance the destruction of the ecosystem to the point where human civilization has entered a phase of collapse? What relationship can be established between this state of affairs and the characteristics of the human psychic system?

The response is relatively simple. Humans are born completely free; their organizational memory has yet to be constituted, and their regulators for abstraction and language have yet to be defined through learning. But they are social beings, formed by society and completely used to following their acquired habits, which Sloterdijk asserts clearly by specifying that human beings are naturally dominated by automatisms [SLO 11]. It is the society in which the human lives that will generate all of this work of forming and structuring their psyche. Human beings will learn to think in certain ways, to memorize and conceive of certain things, to act and react in certain ways depending on their social, economic and cultural circumstances. Their psychic system will be formatted by their education and their everyday life, by what they see and hear. And if we want to understand what is capable of deforming the human psyche's aptitude for adaptability, it is enough to understand the characteristics of the human society that forms and structures them continuously. Thus, we can deduce that the very intricate relationship between the human psyche and the characteristics of human societies has led to downward spirals in dark directions, during which the human easily learns about and conceives of cultural anomalies, such as wars, massacres, slaughters and countless miseries, by enduring them and by enduring the social structures in the world where they almost always exist. The global system, made up of the human with their psyche and all of the structures of human societies that have been constructed, is self-organizing; it is endlessly deployed by being conceived, understood and developed in its organic relationship between humans and societies. So, how can things be changed so that we can finally see things that are always peaceful and beautiful?

Given a meta artificial system that is able to think intentionally, to act according to its intentions by controlling, through networks, innumerable electronic components equipped with a processor that forms its organs, what can such a system do for humans in the thoughts generated by their psyche? We will show the complete model for such a system that is equipped with artificial consciousness, by clearly explaining that although it is a transposition of the human psyche, such a system will not be located in a body but instead will be distributed, and will be a unification of local artificial consciousnesses.

The Computer Representation
of an Artificial Consciousness

We will now describe the computer modeling of a psychic system that generates representations for a system that has an artificial corporeality. That is, an autonomous system that may intentionally generate artificial thoughts and experience them, in accordance with the organizational description of the human psychic system that we detailed in Chapter 1. In this model, we must precisely define how the sensation of thinking is formed in an artificial system and how such an artificial system can experience its idea generation. We will thus demonstrate that there is a relation between the organizational model of human thinking and the model that can be constructed in the field of computer science, which may be programmed and implemented over large distributed corporealities.

We must find out how to represent the generative forms that make up the controllers of the generation of representations in mental landscapes, how to describe the manner in which they are activated, how they reconstitute current mental landscapes, how a representation of a form unifies its components and how this is experienced by the artificial psyche. We will also propose a model with two options. One will be the complete model that begins with an available corporeal form and which will conceptually define all the characteristics of an artificial psyche in order to implement them, starting from the basic elements and defining all knowledge, such as the words in a language and the types of sentences, and all emotions [MAR 07].

Another option will use a corporeality that uses available software to process all the actions of the corporeal form, to apprehend the images of the real world with the identification of objects present here, for the linguistic comprehension of sentences that are heard and the generation of phrases, something that is currently being carried out. For this second option, we must also specify what is required by the system to create the artificial mental representations and, above all, to feel them by experiencing emotions and continuously learning so as to improve its aptitude at generating the correct representations. The key element of the proposed architecture is the coactivity of psychic instances and the unifying management at the informational level, which we call its organizational layer.

We will also show that the general psyche of such an artificial system, when it is distributed over multiple corporeal systems with local artificial consciousnesses, can be unified. And with this, given the power of each artificial psyche, connected with many others and unifying itself with the others to form a meta-system, we are clearly in an area that goes radically beyond the local nature of the human, which poses a major ethical problem to society.

2.1. A multiagent design to generate an artificial psychic system

We must find the right conceptual elements in the field of computer science that make it possible to represent a constructible psychic system related to an artificial corporeal system. The characteristics of the human psyche that we have previously defined commit us to the use of original elements. In effect, any action of the human psyche that generates a mental representation then modifies components in memory, targeting and even modifying the state of the forms of regulation and the mental landscape. This means that it is absolutely impossible to represent the components of an artificial psychic system with multiple algorithms corresponding to functions that operate on components that have permanency and which cannot, thus, be rewritten when in use. When a psyche functions, any action of a regulator that takes into account an aggregate-type component to produce a result modifies the whole system where the initial aggregate was situated, modifies the set of aggregates where the result is produced, modifies the regulator that made it possible to generate the result and also modifies the regulators associated with this action. We must, therefore, abandon the conventional models that are based on functions and move toward a model using computing elements such as lightweight software agents, which can rewrite themselves when in use and which produce systematic modifying effects on the elements of their cognitive classes and on contextual elements for any operation.

We will see that the organization of the lightweight software agents, made up of many agents, can, in a way, represent the generative, scalable forms by defining an organization with elements that represent semantics and others that represent the morphological control over these elements. We must also locally use artificial neural networks to recognize forms, which are the typical feature of these networks, but this would be localized to the action of the specialized software agents.

We can therefore see the central difference between the human psyche and an artificial psyche: the human psyche contains potentialities of elements that are memorized through possible but inactive links between neurons. The activation of these links reactivates the memorized element. The artificial system, however, will contain dormant agents that will be coded and represented as agents, and these must be made to activate themselves in order for the memorized fact to reappear.

We must first return to the use of the first model of the psyche that we discussed, where all the elements are conceptual before being morphological. We cannot, and we will not, be able to directly represent a morphological space made up of multiple lightweight software agents. In the programs that are functioning, the computer generates processes that are executed in sequence or in parallel by processors and which make up the general program that executes the ordered series of its processes. This is the computing reality, there is no neuronal substrate of any kind for processes with a three-dimensional morphology of elements that coactivate each other in parallel. At present, a large amount of research is being carried out on non-digital neuromorphic computers, with the concept of *photonic reservoir computing*, which represent artificial synapses and where the notions of connections and communications are primordial. However, this new type of computer is not yet truly operational for large-scale programs [LAR 12]. We will thus represent morphological activities by continuously simulating the conformations and characteristics of a metric space that describes the activities of clouds of active software agents.

Let us define a lightweight software agent, which is a common feature of artificial intelligence today. We can list the properties of lightweight software agents, seen as design agents, according to Ferber [FER 95]:

– a lightweight software agent is a design and functioning entity that is capable of acting in a planned manner in its environment;

– the agent offers competencies and services;

– the agent possesses limited resources of its own and specific knowledge, represented by some rules or by form recognizers that use neuronal networks;

– the agent is capable of perceiving elements in its environment when provided with just a partial representation of this environment;

– the agent can and must communicate directly with other agents through relationships that are defined at the design stage and which are called acquaintance relationships. These relationships are qualified by going from acquaintances that are favorable to the agent's activities to acquaintances that are unfavorable to the agent's activities;

– the agent is activated by objectives that are unique to it and uses a satisfaction function, or even a survival function and chooses some of the objectives that it seeks to attain, eventually optimizing its choice;

– its behavior tends to satisfy the chosen objectives by taking into account its resources and competencies and depending on its perception of its environments and the communication it receives.

A lightweight agent is therefore a very well-structured software element that has autonomy, is made up of many components and can activate several processes in its functioning. It must be capable of acting without the intervention of another supervisory agent, it is capable of controlling its own actions and its internal state using internal rules that are defined when it is designed, but which may vary. It must have a certain sociability – in other words, it must interact with other agents when the situation requires it in order to amplify its tasks or to help these agents carry out their tasks. In order to do this, it must be proactive.

Proactivity

A proactive element is an element at a conceptual and organizational level that has the ability to act not only in a reactive manner but which has its own goals that it attempts to achieve when it wishes, and that it may revise or modify. The agent thus has local autonomy and is not content with reacting to stimuli by automatically triggering action procedures or an appropriate reaction as is done by objects that systematically activate the corresponding method on receipt of a message. The proactive entity acts on its own account, it assesses the situation in its environment, evaluates the choice of actions it has and, in this sense, it has a certain control over its response and action time.

All lightweight software agents used in the model that we are discussing will be proactive. A multiagent system (MAS) is a system made up of a set of many agents that, through their actions, form an organization. That is, a system that continuously conforms through its actions and relations between active agents to carry out the effective local and global actions. MASs are designed and implemented as a set of agents that interact according to very precise modes of cooperation, with competition, negotiations and opposition; they also, thus, continuously conform their organization so as to bring out the form that allows the most opportune, and often the best-performing, action each time.

Technically, a lightweight software agent has the following seven properties:

1) it is self-centered, i.e. it has its own goals (its reactivity and its proactivity);

2) it is self-motivated (its proactivity);

3) it is interactive (its sociability);

4) it is heterogeneous, i.e. made up of non-homogenous parts (its reactivity, its proactivity and its sociability);

5) it is persistent (its sociability);

6) it is relatively dependent on other agents (its sociability);

7) it can be combined with certain other agents to form a new agent or to generate several others (change in scale in the system).

An MAS is thus characterized by the following properties:

– each agent that is part of it has knowledge and problem-solving abilities that are only partial. It can assess the situation that is local, with respect to the general problem that the MAS must apprehend, manage and resolve with all of its agents;

– there is no global and centralized control in the MAS, which is the major point, because the cooperative activities of the agents form groups and are the site of establishing control at several levels;

– data external to the MAS is taken in through certain interface agents by managing the distribution of this information to other agents;

– the functioning of the global system is carried out by the MAS through the management of the coordination of all of its agents in order to allow for the emergence of a set of active agents that will resolve the current problems in an ongoing manner.

All the knowledge given to the agents come from ontologies that are predefined to characterize the system and its behaviors [DEC 12]. With all these characteristics, the problem will indeed be that of defining the agents that constitute the artificial psychic system and carrying out a continuous control of the MAS so that it regularly generates coherent and satisfactory emergences. The system to be constructed has a functional substrate that specifies the functional actions of a well-defined artificial corporeal system. All the necessary knowledge is provided by the ontologies that specify the functionality of all the elements in this corporeal system and all that the system must do in everyday situations. This makes it possible to manipulate cognitive categories in the conventional sense of information processing. We will, thus, have the following cognitive categories:

– characteristics of space and duration for the system's corporal actions;

– characteristics of the description of any object taken into account by the corporeality sensors, vision sensors at all levels and sound sensors;

– use of cognitive types to characterize all the objects apprehended: constructed, living, natural, structured, composite, mobile, interesting, unknown, dangerous, etc.

– representing cognitive knowledge defined by conceptual elements, words being able to form sentences, then abstract knowledge of large scientific fields such as physics, linguistics, psychology, etc.;

– developing internal communication to interlink all the manipulated knowledge: creating multiple multilevel cognitive networks, with cognitive operations that generate new subnetworks;

– operators to manipulate knowledge to carry out analyses and syntheses such as: generalizing, specifying, extracting, assembling, unifying, breaking up, etc.

All available knowledge must be represented in numerous classes of software agents so that it becomes dynamic and may be used in the activity of the system of agents. The initial knowledge of all cognitive data and everything that the system must necessarily carry out, with precise conditions, will be represented in specific agents, which will reify them. We then speak of **design agents** [CAR 16]. A design agent is a lightweight agent that will represent some specific knowledge, a particular aspect of a thing, a structural sign, an indication about a specific situational question or a partial result in the form of a response to a given question. The organization of the agents represents this local knowledge and must therefore produce significant aggregations of agents in order for the knowledge to compose itself and become more pertinent. For instance, a piece of information is produced by interface agents on signs observed in the environment, then the design agents connected with the interface agents generate questions related to the information provided by these agents and their eventual pertinence; the emergence of appropriate and relevant responses to this questioning causes the design agents to act and process the knowledge. Any design agent can, thus, correspond with the semantic character of an ontological form that can be deployed in cognitive operations.

A design agent must have the following classic structure:

– name identifying the agent;

– the specific ontological category of the agent and the more general category that it inherits;

– the current state of the agent, with current tendency;

– messaging in reading and broadcast;

– rules for actions that can be carried out that may modify themselves;

– meta-rules governing the activities and rules, which can be modified;

– qualified and progressive positive acquaintances;

– qualified and progressive negative acquaintances;

– the agent's memory, which is progressive.

We are within a framework where the knowledge used matters only when activated in groups that are organized with their relational evolutions, in transformations that turn the system into a very scalable form of dynamic organization. The agents that have factual knowledge communicate with other agents to give them indications on the cognitive aspects, eventually via communication agents that carry out these relational operations. The agents that receive the knowledge will make use of it and eventually modify the knowledge. The MAS's action no longer has fixed structures that are available as databases, instead there are multiple organizations of agents that are coactive. There will be design agents reifying basic knowledge with their multiple specific relations. There will then be other agents operating on the knowledge expressed by the design agents, which will use cognitive relations by making the knowledge cooperate: unifying groups, separating into different subgroups, reinforcing, weakening, changing relations to improve efficiency, etc.

We also have agents that will carry out semantic and morphological control on the activities of the groups of design agents. These are called the **regulation agents** [CAR 09]. Regulation agents correspond to the regulators, which were presented in Chapter 1.

Let us specify the essential properties of a regulation agent. The lightweight software agents will be classified across multiple cognitive categories and, through rules and meta-rules, will reify and apply precise and local knowledge to the organized functioning of groups of design agents so that they can be organized based on their semantic characteristics. Each design agent's activity reveals local functional and cognitive aspects of the system as being pertinent in its own domain and will not refer to the general situation of the system. In order to express the pertinence of the knowledge that it represents, this agent must systematically connect with other agents. Thus, most importantly, it will have the property of contextually placing its knowledge and orienting it globally, guided in a specific way by the action of the regulation agents that supervise it and represent control, and all the tendencies of the functioning of the system in its context. The design agent will therefore never be reduced to an automatic and isolated mechanical symbol but will be an organization entity that places itself in an action position with other agents to form groups with the motivational local supervision of regulation agents in order to participate in the emergence of the representation. The regulation agent will possess semantic information on the groups of agents that it is supervising, and morphological and geometric information specifying the characteristics of the categories and forms of these groups. It can generate this information internally in order to use it.

2.2. Designing the artificial psychic system using a multiagent approach

An artificial system capable of generating forms of thoughts will differ from the human psyche in several ways. The artificial system must be conceived of as having an operational consciousness, as it does not develop in the progressive manner of humans, where, from early childhood onwards, the human learns to conceive of increasingly complex thoughts. It will not learn to speak from nothing and will not learn to recognize objects if it knows nothing. It will be endowed with clearly defined knowledge when it is constructed and this will allow it to know elements of language and multiple things from the visible real world. This is an artificial system that will be relatively operational when it starts functioning and, of course, it can and must evolve a lot. It will, thus, have an operational base and learning aptitudes. Setting it into operation means that it will have the autonomy to act and understand its environment and that it may learn by improving its knowledge. Thus, the conceptual elements that allow it to think will be elements that do what the neural aggregates do, by organizing themselves and by creating new organizations, which could represent organizational memory and tendencies. The organizational design of the human psyche that we have defined will help in carrying out the transposition required to do this.

The generation of artificial thoughts requires that the system that will produce these thoughts is considered as essentially being dynamic, deploying its reorganizations that intentionally produce representations by basing themselves on a very architectural corporeality with the ability to apprehend this corporeality and the environment. Such a system must endlessly reconform in multiple manners on different scales and depending on the goals. The categories of elements that form its continuous constructions of representations must represent aggregate forms on multiple levels, in continual reconstructions, holding good for events or things that can be conceptualized that the system will assess.

There is no initial notion of state in the production of such a system (which is, however, in the field of computer sciences), a state that would lead to a final state, which would be that of the generated thought. It is a system with dynamic architecture, as is the brain, which is always modifying its physical structure and which will be able to assess its configurations using sensations. Its operating principle is the constructive modification of its state, which is organized to generate and attain certain physical conformations that will be specific and satisfactory representations of the apprehended things. But this is a system in the organizational sense of the term, i.e. an organization of components, with an interior, a membrane and an exterior; the membrane is the informational level provided by the multiple sensors in the corporeality [VAR 89].

The system will have the same major components as the model of the psychic system that we presented earlier and will thus have five instances: an emotional system, an unconscious, a preconscious, a conscious and an organizational layer, which will carry out the major role of coactive multiscale control of the system and which correspond to the systemic layer.

The system will thus have an artificial corporeality that allows it to apprehend elements of the real world, images and sounds for example. This is today carried out by sensors whose information is finely processed and produces data sent to an object layer. It will have multiple artificial organs to move its physical elements over the ground, or spatially, and others to grasp objects. This corporeality will be a physical substrate made of a large number of different electronic and mechanical components, which will always communicate with information transfer in both directions: toward the artificial psychic system for analysis and the command of the organs of the corporeality. All these elements of the corporeality have their own functionalities and continuity of functions and form a substrate in well-specified functional domains. When creating the system, the set of components of the physical substrate and their functional relations are interpreted at the level of the basic information and form the **object layer on the substrate**, something an automation engineer can do perfectly. These object layers are distributed, based on the functional applications, with a distribution that eventually becomes peer-to-peer or client-server [CLO 00]. The system that represents the artificial consciousness can use this substrate permanently to apprehend information from the environment and experience corporeal sensations, which allows it to engage in actions.

We must therefore define all the significant elements that characterize the things that the system will apprehend from the perceived real world through its sensors and which it will use to form some of its representations. These elements will be given by the multiple ontologies of the domains, something that is very precisely developed today. What will then be needed is to create design agents that will use them, which is more specific.

We must define an emotional center that is capable of generating the usual emotions such as surprise, pleasure, astonishment and very strong emotions such as fear or anguish. These will be regulated by the system's consciousness so that the system does not spend too long in a period where it does not control its thought productions. Thus, cognitive ontologies developed in psychology relating to emotional processes will be used to better structurally represent these in order to agentify them.

The ontologies and categorizations that use the concepts of the knowledge level for all things that the system may know will establish the link between the perceptible real world and the constructed representations. All the ontologies and all the knowledge of perceptible reality must be transposed into the elements that make up an essentially dynamic system based on a certain method and allow it to use the concepts and knowledge used, in the correct form and the right scale. This is the **agentification of knowledge** of the system.

The design agents must represent all elements of knowledge that make it possible to define the constitutive characteristics of the artificial emotions and thoughts. They thus contain all information and knowledge on objects and events of reality, all the words of the language and the characteristics of types of sentences to form them. All this forms a cognitive set that is very large in size, with a very large number of defined agents. The action carried out by these agents forms the basis for all representations that will be generated. The system will, of course, have the aptitude to continuously integrate new knowledge in the form of new design agents, to combine new agents to form more coherent sets, to transform the older organizations of the agents. But if the system does not possess a very good initial knowledge base, it will never be truly high performing nor very operational. We can observe that knowledge of this kind has long been accumulated and structured in the humanities, in philosophy and in cognitive sciences in all fields and the computer scientists creating the system must use this knowledge. This knowledge must be agentified in order to make it the cognitive foundation of the system that will produce the artificial thoughts. This agentification is quite heavy work, which must make it possible to transpose static knowledge (such as the knowledge of dictionaries and corpuses) into a dynamic universe founded on relations between active elements. We will, thus, base ourselves on the existence of the numerous ontologies that are currently available to create the numerous design agents required, using well-adapted interfacing tools.

Any characteristic element in the cognitive field representing a character that describes a state, a value, a concept, a structure, a form, a movement, a typical or causal relation or even an evolution along a certain point of view will always be represented by several design agents. This therefore places this knowledge within different frameworks, illuminating different points of view expressed by the agents. A design agent is the behavioral general of the dynamic knowledge that it represents, functioning within the organization of the active knowledge as a local element that can make itself significant through its aggregation negotiated with other active agents.

The design agents thus represent all the characteristics with the local and more general (even global) effects of the functionalities described by the behavior of all things that can be apprehended. The effects and the changes in the characteristics or the aspects of the apprehended objects are systematically represented by agents that have the ability to activate themselves, communicate and, above all, form aggregates of agents that generate the aspect of a certain subject.

We can define design agents that have a general role relative to certain classes and certain types of actions from the knowledge produced by using the ontologies. The field of this type of agent is a particular ontological subclass in the general typology. A specific design agent of a specific type may be generated by a reification carried out by an agent of a more general type, by placing the new agent against a characterization with respect to a particular element under consideration. It will be produced by specialized generalization starting from an agent of a slightly more general type, with an ontological field bearing particular aspects, over particular cases or particular elements. Thus, a new subclass is created in the hierarchy of ontologies.

The behavior of a design agent is governed by the "linear decision" process, which was inspired by the concept of decision, developed by Lucien Sfez [SFE 92]. This has been precisely defined in another work [CAR 12]. The behavioral progression of such an agent is carried out by passing through steps corresponding to those of the decision, said to be linear. In other words, the behavior of a design agent is based on a macro-automaton representing the state of its proactivity, that is, an automaton where each state is also an automaton. This macro-automaton has four states. These are initialization, deliberation, decision and action. Each time the design agent moves from one of these states to another, it is plunged into the automaton of the corresponding state having its own rules of activity driven by its specific meta-rules.

Design agents thus act in the following manner:

1) input of information from the elements on their local environment: other connected agents or objects in their context or information from the system interface;

2) the rational interpretation of this information depending on the local contexts and the internal tendencies present when using appropriate rules;

3) the production of action plans, adapted with prior evaluation (if needed) of the actions envisaged, using meta-rules;

4) the choice of a precise action plan and engaged action;

5) effective external action with the transmission of messages, generation of objects or agents to appropriate receptors. Or even order the effectors of the artificial organism to act on the corporeality or in the memory;

6) an appropriate modification of the internal state of the agent through this activity, with memorization and adaptation of rules and qualifications of acquaintances;

7) the evaluation of results of the action carried out and qualitative memorization.

It may be considered that we have the software to manage the corporeality, to process the images of the environment and identify the objects that figure here, as well as other pieces of software that process the comprehension and enunciation of speech and sentences. We posit, of course, that these different pieces of software are not closed and that it is possible to use them by intervening in some of their functioning procedures. What remains to be defined in this case is the upper layer of the psychic system, which generates the artificial mental representations and which feels them, experiences them and then memorizes them in synthetic form.

Here again we will be using design and regulation agents, but on a more specific level. We will define a system that uses and controls the corporeality, that uses the results of the image processing and speech comprehension, and that controls the enunciation of sentences.

We thus have the following two-part scheme for the flow of algorithmic steps. The first is the use of specific software that have already been created and the second is the generation of the representations that will be experienced:

– **Part concerning use of specific software**

    - activity of the corporeality's control and analysis elements;

    - analysis of the images from the environment: list of identified objects and the structured state of this environment;

    - activity of the auditory system and system for the interpretation of sentences heard;

    - system for precise localization within an identifier environment;

    - system defining the local intentions based on behavioral tendencies;

- system controlling the image-processing software: what are the interesting objects? And the potential search for certain objects, proximities and details;

- system controlling the software of the interpretation of sentences heard: who is speaking and about what? What are the themes and the tone?

– Specific part to be developed

- system defining the mental landscape based on knowledge of the contextual situation with the deployment of design agents;

- system defining the current goal with intention and knowledge of the situation;

- system generating the current representation;

- system experiencing the representation, feeling it as an act of artificial thought;

- system engaging in behavioral action;

- system engaging in pursuing activity with the production of representations.

This kind of system therefore uses the results of specific software and defines the architecture of the psychic system that carries out the intentional generation of goals and experiences the generated representation in a sensible manner. We are thus very near the general case and only the processing of specific points by well-adapted software will be used. What remains, thus, is to define the architecture of this system that generates goals with intention and experiences what it generates as the representation of thought.

2.3. Self-control of the artificial psychic system using regulator agents

When the design agents taken from the set of many defined design agents are activated, the central development of the system will control them. The concept of *regulation agent* will be used to establish this control. This is similar to the concept of regulator, introduced in the first part, and will be a type of controller that makes it possible to manage every level of the numerous relations between all active design agents. This concept of regulation manages the many levels where the set of design agents are active and thus makes it possible to define tendencies for the generation of representations and to generate these representations by specifying many characters. This was the point to be identified in the use of massive MAS. We will thus define the regulation agents in order to represent emotions, basic needs, feelings, sociability, aptitude for abstraction, reasoning, judgement, questioning, generalization, classification, quality and the depth of memorization. All these agents will operate through incentive control over the design agents so that the semantic aspects represented by the aggregates of these agents adapt to the desired qualitative characters by coming together in certain ways to constitute the conformations.

Let us specify what a regulation agent is.

Regulation agent

A regulation agent is a controller that operates through incentives on the design agents and on the groups of design agents in order to make them take on certain semantic characters to organize them with the categorization of these characters, knowing that the design agents are proactive and activate themselves in order to achieve their goals, first and foremost. These regulation agents represent the concept of the regulator used in the human psychic system. There will, necessarily, be multiple regulation agents operating on numerous levels to represent all necessary regulation categories. If desired, the regulation agents can ontologically represent "qualitative action verbs", describing all that is action, either real or virtual, which can be expressed in a representation, as the design agents are the semantic aspects of this scene of action. The regulation agents form an organized space as they also operate on themselves, in order to coordinate themselves, associate themselves and differentiate themselves into different sets and to modify themselves through self-learning.

The distinction employed here between verb and noun or adjective was used in R. Thom's work on the representation of language and the system of thought [THO 90]. Thus, if desired, the regulation agents can be designed from verbs to use and organize all the expressive and descriptive aspects represented intermittently by the design agents. Such an agent describes an action and is itself the action to construct the organized elements of a representation.

The general computational structure of a regulation agent is very close to the structure of the design agent that we have discussed and the characteristics of its knowledge and of its action rules change drastically.

The structure of a regulation agent is as follows:

– the name identifying the regulation agent;

– the specific ontological class of the agent;

– the current state of the agent, with the expression of its active tendency;

– messaging in reading and broadcast toward the design agents;

– messaging in reading and broadcast toward the regulation agents;

– list of design agents specifically expressing the characteristics of its ontological class;

– rules for actions carried out on the design agents;

– rules for actions carried out on the regulation agents:

– meta-rules governing the activities and all the rules, especially for connections with the other regulation agents;

– qualified and progressive positive acquaintances with the design agents to be used;

– qualified and progressive negative acquaintances with the opposing design agents;

– qualified and progressive positive acquaintances with the friendly regulation agents;

– qualified and progressive negative acquaintances with the opposing regulation agents;

– the agent's memory, which is highly evolving.

These agents thus have the list of acquaintances of design agents that represent the reification of their characters and which they will then activate and closely survey, as well as other lists of design agents that strongly oppose their characters, which will also be supervised.

The action of a regulation agent is rational and it is carried out in cooperation with the other active regulation agents. The actions are as follows:

– analyzing the morphological structure of a group of active design agents based on the semantic characters that they express. Revealing the pertinent characters of this structure by comparing this to its central ontological theme to see whether the group can be used in its search for the correct representatives of its theme, by modifying them to a lesser or greater degree;

– analyzing the state of action and influence of the other regulation agents to define the current degree of freedom of its ontological class;

– attempting, under conditions, to amplify or reduce certain groups of design agents by eventually calling upon other regulation agents to cooperate and obtain help by broadening or specializing the general semantics that will characterize the supervised and controlled group;

– memorizing the result of its action for systematic learning.

The regulation agents activate certain groups of design agents based on their ontological characters and, above all, they alter the behaviors of these groups in their ontological intention and in relation to the actions of other regulation agents. They cause groups that are specific to their theme to activate themselves in cooperation with other regulation agents to represent the right characters in the conformations generated for representation, including all the nuances of affectivity in the form of the conformations, intensity and speed of the actions of the groups. The feature of these controllers is that they are distributed and operate with a very high degree of coactivity through a continuous exchange of information. They will not make up classic hierarchic structures of control but only define an evolving control that is adaptive in nature. That is, they govern the manner in which design agents must aggregate themselves by influencing others to finally produce a geometrically and semantically admissible form. This defines an original concept of emergence in self-controlled systems. We can also say that the groups of design agents are **aggregates of agents** that have one semantic expression and one geometric conformation, like neuronal aggregates.

Regulation agents are elements whose activation is defined in the control spaces, allowing them to globally alter clouds of design agent aggregates, simultaneously and on different scales. At this level, they form force lines that majorly influence the activity of the system of agents. These incentive control elements, reified in the form of regulation agents, represent the tendencies, habits and, aptitudes for rational reasoning and for symbolization; and the social and cultural tendencies of the system through the manipulation of the design agents specific to these characters or that are related to these characters. They are significant in the system architecture and operate as the reification of an organizational field.

The regulation agents dynamically represent the ontological hierarchies of the system's knowledge. There are general regulation agents like those that indicate positive emotion, for example, and then there are more specific agents that are derived from this, such as those indicating desire or satisfaction. We thus have morphologies of the regulation agents, forming (if so desired) ontological classes that are related through semantic distances and controlling well-adapted design agents. These morphologies must be managed and this is what we will discuss later in the chapter.

There are several regulation agents to represent all the possible characters of the representations. The problem here will be to activate only some of them to form a coherent set with precise characteristics. In order to do this, we must introduce the concept of mental landscape into the agentified system, which will make it possible to define a set of active regulation agents in all instances to produce series of representations in a specific atmosphere.

The goal of the system, with its artificial corporeality, will be to generate coherent action plans and to act. It must then review the planning based on the results in order to improve it, to always continue learning to produce representations that are ever more detailed. This means that the system will use regulation agents that are well adapted to this objective, regulation agents that strive to produce representations of the critiques, the analyses and the questioning, that ensure that all the results of this process will be in coherence and that ensure the good performance of the organizational memory, whose role will be absolutely critical.

2.4. The organizational architecture of the system

We thus have a system that has a corporeality made up of multiple electromechanical devices and the artificial psychic system, which is essentially a computerized system, receives multiple information from the sensors of this corporeality. The psychic system must also have an organizational memory, where an enormous amount of knowledge can be localized in the form of design agents and regulation agents to represent forms of memories that have been apprehended. Depending on its habits and tendencies, the system will ceaselessly construct representations by activating its design agents controlled by its regulation agents, which will engage it in action with its corporeality. To generate representations, the system must engage in the process that constructs it and this begins with the specification of a thematic indication that we call **the aim of a representation**.

The aim of a representation

Any representation is generated from a thematic indication, the aim of the representation that commits the system to deploying elements to support this indication, to construct the form of the produced and apprehended representation. The indication that will result in the process of constructing the representation is either intentional (and is derived from the action of the regulation agents that make the decisional intention in the conscious system) or arises from regulation agents who represent tendencies and desires and in this case a representation

> is produced that conforms to the thematic indication of the desire and the state of the mental landscape, strongly using the experience that has expressed the action of this very tendency in similar cases. Any representation is also an element in a more or less large series of local representations that are perceived.

The architecture of the system generating the representations will be as follows, deduced from the architecture presented for the human psychic system, with numerous subsystems, which, in this case, will be localized but very well connected and will represent the instances where clouds of software agents will be active (see Figure 2.1):

– the **corporeality of the system**: this is a set of a large number of sensors and effectors connected in a continuous manner to a specific object layer that takes all the information, then to the design agents of the interface that interpret the information, making it possible to represent and interpret the input of the informational flow coming from the environment, in a manner that is consistent with the usual practice. Taking into account all these sensory sensors, data must be gathered on an ongoing basis for the object layers that will send them to the interface agents. These interface agents in turn will process the data and evaluate it quantitatively and then qualitatively in order to find out whether an immediate automatic reaction must be launched or whether the data should be sent to the emotion processing system to produce representations; or, if the data are habitual, normal, they are not taken into account in the representations;

– an **emotion processing system** generates emotions in response to data coming from the corporeality and to fundamental tendencies. This important component is, of course, related to the corporeality and also the components of the preconscious and the unconscious, with which it ceaselessly communicates by making their multiple regulation agents communicate between themselves. It manages the formation and development of emotions so that they are experienced well and sensations lead to feelings. It can generate aims related to very subjective or cognitive desires. The sensors and emotion-processing center will always remain active in order to represent the sensibility of the artificial organism. The data from the corporeality will be seen as a continuous flow of information, some of which brings about automatic physical reactions of the "reflex" type. Any failure in the physical elements of the corporeality will be perceived as sensations of pain or even functional anomalies;

– an **unconscious system**, made up of groups of dormant design agents and regulation agents, represents all the knowledge and all the naturally or artificially experienced events. By localizing the large **organizational memory**, it also organizes – through multiple dynamic networks where the memory regulation agents will operate – the design agents that reify all the knowledge and memories of the system. The unconscious system will also localize the regulation agents that represent the artificial impulses as those generating desires;

– a **preconscious system** that is, in the functioning of the system, made up of an organization of clouds of active design agents, with agents interpreting information from the sensory sensors and the elements transferred from the unconscious during the launch of activity with the aim of providing elements of pre-representations. This system will generate the pre-representations, which will evolve. It plays a major role in the representation of the current mental landscape made up of the coordinated set of active regulators that fix the current characters of the system. This preconscious will be associated with an immediate memory, localizing the perennially pertinent activities for the streams of ongoing emergences;

– a **conscious system** that ensures the complete formation of the current representation through the construction of an emerging coherent form, by choosing one or more pre-representations in the preconscious system. The conscious system has a very specific subsystem that expresses the **sensation of thinking** through multicriteria analysis of the conformation of the representation in order to produce a memory synthesis. This component can gather and apprehend the characters of the pre-representations of the preconscious system and calls upon one (or an association of several) of these to develop them and create the current representation. It enforces the intentional aims to produce representations which cause the regulation agents to activate themselves in all instances and especially in the organizational layer and in the preconscious system, which will develop the representations along the theme of the aim. The conscious system will thus have the role of controlling the emergences and also a role of arousal for that which may emerge, by producing aims;

– an **immediate memory system** that makes it possible to localize what was just experienced in the conscious, which will be finely associated with the preconscious, influence the formation of| pre-representations and will then place well-structured elements into the organizational memory;

– an **organizational layer**, the equivalent of the systemic layer, which makes it possible to establish a link between the emotion center, the unconscious, the preconscious and the conscious, and which makes it possible to give the system organizational coherence. This informational layer is strongly coordinated with the conscious system in order to diffuse the aim and generate the correct pre-representations. This is a general informational layer, a distributed network using its own regulation agents that will thus cause regulation agents to activate themselves in all instances by realizing their homogeneity. This layer will produce the **mental landscape** by causing the regulation agents to activate themselves in a coordinated manner where these agents will be coherent in all instances, thus producing, in each instance, its specific characters and unifying them in order for the action of the regulation agents to create a climate of representation to be managed. Its regulation agents will thus play a major coordinating role by controlling the aggregates of agents in the other instances. A conscious system could play a steering role, through its regulation agents, as a part of this layer connects the preconscious to the conscious in order to impose the current aim with its tendencies. The organizational layer that reifies the mental landscape will thus lead to the activation of the correct agents of regulation of instances to carry out the development of the pre-representations according to the aim. In the context of the mental landscape, the regulation agents of the instances will cause the correct design agents to extract themselves at the right time and at the right sites to allow for their coherent and appropriate aggregation in the preconscious, then to place the correct representation in the conscious so that it is finalized.

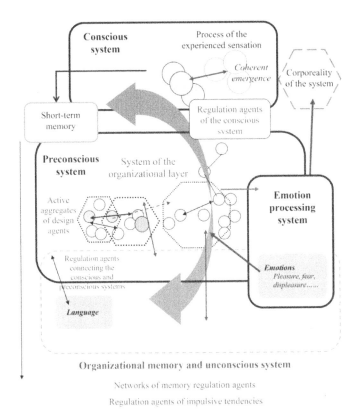

Figure 2.1. *Organizational scheme of the artificial psychic system.*
For a color version of the figure, please see www.iste.co.uk/cardon/ai.zip

In the artificial psychic system, the agents are relatively mobile between instances and are especially coactive in order to produce organized aggregates, the whole being driven by regulation agents of the organizational layer, the role of its agents being, above all, that of controlling regulation agents of instances, which in turn chiefly control the design agents. Thus, the design agents and regulation agents will form coherent, dynamic morphologies, variable, interconnected and changing, but typical of the characters of different instances. These morphologies are, geometrically, conformations with one or more dominant elements at the energetic and conceptual level, and they will, thus, often be lattice-type sets, with elements associated in variable relations of association or domination. The ensemble will be definable based on the relational, conceptual and energetic dimensions and there will be specific regulation agents for studies of the morphologies of the aggregates of agents to characterize them and give the regulation agents the correct indications for their morphological and semantic characters.

Status of the computable architecture of the artificial psychic system

> The computable architecture of the artificial psychic system defines a very dynamic organization, which has subsystems that represent the five instances of a psychic system, and which makes it possible, using a high number of agents and structures of agents defined at the construction, to realize emergent representations that are stable for an instant, cognitive and sensible, with precise roles for generating thoughts and deepening knowledge. Such an architecture will have the property of being able to evaluate its emergent representations formed of agents by the system that represents the instance of the conscious, which is the process that corresponds to the sensation of thinking and it can, thus, question the internal constructs of its organizational memory to deploy its questioning in an intentional manner.

These different systems that represent the instances cooperate to a high degree with the regulation agents, but they operate with enough autonomy to define the essential characters of the system. They are coordinated by the organizational layer, which is the control layer deployed over all the specific systems and whose regulation agents carry out the control. As the control of the regulation agents is not imperative but realized with incitement and needs to be established and re-established, to be re-formulated and to be adapted, the system will be very flexible. To remedy the inconsistencies between opposing regulation agents, we will use meta regulation agents in the organizational layer, something that does not exist very clearly in the human psychic system, but which can be easily installed in the artificial system.

The concept of regulation agent is central to this architecture, as they will be regulators of instances and will define organized functioning in the system. The architecture will make it possible to define the tendencies to intentionally produce representations and, above all, to define the particular types of representations. There will, thus, be regulation agents to represent the different emotions, sentiments, sociability, aptitudes for abstraction, reasoning, judgment, the quality of memorizations, questioning, abstraction, generalization, classification and the problem will be that of coordinating these aptitudes and organizing their morphology. The structuring agent that makes it possible to define the control of the aggregates of the design agents in the system by the regulation agents is presented in Figure 2.2.

The integrated morphological and
temporal organization

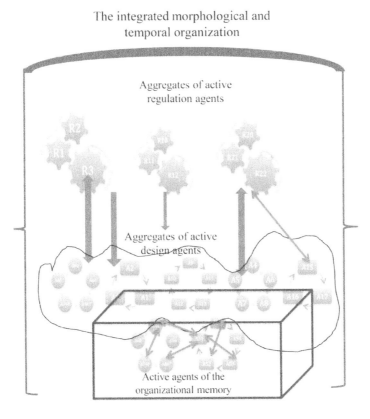

Figure 2.2. *The agent architecture for the control of design agent aggregates. For a color version of the figure, please see www.iste.co.uk/cardon/ai.zip*

With this system architecture, there will be three categories of regulation agents depending on their placement in the relations between the systems that represent the instances:

1) the regulation agents that operate at the level of the relation between the unconscious and the preconscious via the organizational layer carry out their own activity outside the conscious and define deep tendencies. These controllers will thus reify the impulsive tendencies and cause memories to activate themselves depending on the theme of the aim and depending on the active tendencies;

2) the regulation agents operating at the level of the conscious–unconscious link via the organizational layer, which will be those that make it possible to generate the thought representations and effectively exercise the concepts of reason and will of the system, and, doing so, to deploy the pre-representations in the mental landscapes;

3) the regulation agents operating in the conscious to intentionally define the aim, to seize upon the pre-representation and act on it to form the representation, to generate apprehension and the sensation of thinking, which will construct a synthesis of this representation placed in the immediate memory system by dissolving the representation and freeing its constituent agents.

The regulation agents that link the preconscious to the unconscious will act in the following fields in particular, through calls and by activating the appropriate agents in the organizational memory by wrapping them to construct aggregates depending on their specific characters:

– classifications and categorizations, types of reasoning, logical manipulations, classifications and distinctions, structuring knowledge, types of emotions and sensations, postural elements, temporal characters, spatial characters, abstractions, designations, identifications and knowledge, types of shapes and movements, all the language categories, geometric categories, judgements and assessments, typical humor, social rules, deep or acquired tendencies, learning, important events, etc.

In the regulation agents that connect the conscious and the preconscious, there are agents operating on the aggregated proposed to the conscious, making it possible to realize the sensation of thinking, but also acting on the expression of regulation agents of the preconscious to invest them and modify their behaviors depending on the current mental landscape and goal. These regulation agents in the conscious will have corresponding types in the regulation agents of the preconscious but these will have deeper actions. Their principal types of actions may be:

– questioning and curiosity, sensible tonality and feelings, posture and choice of posture, reflections on the structuring of knowledge, realism and questioning of habit, fundamental perception of being, the feeling of existing, sensation of temporality, deep values, judgements (including moral judgements), fundamental values and ethics, apprehension of self and the other, fundamental categories, safeguarding the integrity of the system, etc.

All these actions will take into account knowledge very finely placed in organizational memory and which makes it possible to carry out analyses and memorize their results in a well-organized form and not simply as a list of things.

The conscious will also have regulation agents that engage in the intentional generation of aims. This will form an organization of agents that define, each time, a dominant regulation agent that will give the character of the aim and pledge in the activation of regulation agents that conform to the character indicated by this aim throughout the system. There will also be regulation agents engaging in producing a certain mental landscape, that is, activating certain types of regulation agents in all other instances and causing the immediate activation of design agents that express the specific characters of this type, notably by extracting them from the organizational memory using the regulation agents of the memory to place them in the preconscious. The mental landscape will be in place before the generation of the aim, which makes it possible to produce series of representations around a single theme and it may be transformed by specific regulation agents of this action by changing the context and type of aim.

The organizational layer will localize a meta regulation agent, the highly important **regulation agent of intentionality**, operating on the morphology of the space of the regulation agents and making it possible to continuously define free will in the choice of aims. Its action will be divided between the conscious and the organizational layer. This is in opposition to the autonomous generation of aims by the regulation agents of fundamental tendencies, which will produce desires for things arising from the context or the organizational memory.

We will now proceed to a detailed examination of the organizational memory, which is the major system that makes it possible to memorize experiences and introduce facts that constitute the forms of the representations.

2.5. Organizational memory and artificial experience

The system has a memory that contains dynamic and well-structured knowledge, with the memorization of events that have been experienced, apprehended and perceived. This makes it a memory that does not at all operate by selecting information that has been requested but which contains multiple small networks describing the aggregates of design agents representing the memorization of phenomena that have been apprehended. The use of the memorization of experienced events is fundamental to producing sensible representations. The production of any artificial thought will be based on the use of a memorized experience and used by the flow of the expression of tendencies and desires represented by the regulation agents. The constitution of this experience, its precise architecture and its manipulation, which must be very efficient, are one of the keys to the realization of the system of generation of artificial thoughts.

The organizational memory of the system will have the following structure. At the level of the representation of the memory elements, it is composed of specific design agents, the **memory design agents**, which have the following structure:

– the memory agent has an identifier, an ontological domain and a very precise theme;

– it represents a character of a representation that has been generated;

– it indicates its ontological field, which is a character like a sentence-word, an image that has been apprehended, the context of an event, the circumstances of a sensation or a feeling that has been perceived, etc. These characters are represented in the memory agent by a short list that names the specific design agents, which have these characters and comes from the memorized representation. These are direct indications of the identity of these agents, which is the normal choice for coding in order not to use design agents multiple times. As we will see, this will also be a choice of conformity with the case of the living being;

– in addition to its particular ontological class, it indicates the ontological hierarchy that situates its theme;

– it specifies its importance through the frequency of its use;

– there are three types of lists of principal acquaintances: the memory design agents that have characters close to their own, memory agents that have a more general theme than their own and memory agents that have subordinate themes and which are specialized in their theme. The memory design agent thus indicates its position in the conceptual and ontological hierarchy of memorized facts;

– it indicates the memory agents of a different class but which are often activated following its own activation, which are in another hierarchy or which may indeed be close to it but have formed aggregates of agents active with it, which makes it possible to clearly define the characters of the experience;

– it has a memory that indicates the employment of its uses and its modifications.

Such an agent is therefore a factual indicator of a memorized event and is, above all, an operator who specifies the three possible operations on its theme: completing the theme, generalizing it or specializing it. It is thus a character representing a fact that intervenes in a memorized representation and which will engage the eventual activity of the three chief ontological operations of the organizational memory that we previously described and which are the basic set-theoretic operations.

The organizational memory will be organized into networks of memory agents related through concepts of semantic proximities or semantic generalizations. The concepts of proximity, specialization and generalization can be precisely defined using qualifications related to the acquaintances of the agents.

Furthermore, the difference between the immediate memory and the organizational memory is thus very clear. Immediate memory preserves the conformations of the representations made by the design agents, which renders its elements immediately operational. In the case of organizational memory, we must extract graphs whose elements are indicators for the agents and reconstitute the aggregates of design agents to activate them, which takes much longer.

This organizational memory can then be very precisely qualified in different domains, certain of them being specific to sensible facts and others to conceptual and rational facts that qualify many different domains. This will be managed, at the general level, by **memory regulation agents**, which are also called **memory indicator agents**, which will form an indicative memory layer over all the memory design agents. These regulation agents will solicit the parts of the memory where the memory design agents are available by identifying them based on their characters. They will also be the interface agents for the organizational memory in communication with the other regulation agents of other instances.

Memory regulation agent

A **memory regulation agent** is used to indicate the memorized elements to activate them based on semantic characters and the manipulation events that identify them. Each agent of this type belongs to a general ontological class and indicates the very specific subclass of that which it could precisely reference, very often with temporal and contextual instructions. It is therefore a thematic indicator and has lists of memory design agents that specify the semantic characters corresponding to its own and those that are semantically close or a little removed from it. These agents will indicate either precise memory design agents or sets of memory design agents that form the complete memorization of a set of representations of neighboring themes. They can also modify the characters and structures of memory design agents, in the case of insertion of a new representation into the memory. These will be accessible to regulation agents of other instances that will solicit them, which can activate them to trigger the onset of a memory either of a piece of knowledge or an event.

We have specified that the regulation agents of instances have precise ontological characters and have lists of acquaintances that indicate to them the memory regulation agents that have the same ontological character or ontological characters that are close or opposing. The regulation agents will form the **informational layer of the organizational memory**, which defines a network of semantic and morphological relations between all the elements, between them and with the memory design agents.

In order to make this memory high performing, we thus have memory regulation agents that indicate the theme defined in the ontologies by referring to more specific memory regulation agents. This is done at all levels of the ontological instructions and these will thus be indicative controllers of the characters borne by the memory regulation agents. We thus have an informational layer that organizes this memory and, based on a character of any given level of input by a regulation agent of the other instances, there will be automatic querying carried out between the memory regulation agents to arrive at the correct group of memory design agents.

The memory design agents are small structures that indicate the form and content of the memorized representation in the form of graphs. In these graphs, the nodes are the indicators for the design agents, the arcs indicate the semantics of the relations and the amplitude of semantic distances, and the facets of the graphs represent the geometric forms of the memorized morphological conformation, with peaks and necessary subordinate forms. There is also an indication of the major element in this graph, corresponding to the central theme of the memorized representation, then the relative value of the set of nodes. The organizational memory, in its entirety, is thus a very large graph of graphs with multiple domains that must be manipulated and whose semantic distances must be indicated. And here, the memory regulation agents will be absolutely necessary as they are the dynamic pathways to go from a graph with semantics to its subgraphs and, finally, to the set of memory design agents that had to be identified. These paths are learnt and memorized in the memory regulation agents, which communicate between themselves. The memory regulation agents thus form an informational layer of manipulation of the graph of graphs, which is itself a set that has the characters of the informational graphs.

Thus, any regulation agent of an instance that solicits the organizational memory acts in the following manner:

– definition of the character to be solicited taken from the aim or from the aggregates of design agents in an instance like the preconscious;

– action of the regulation agent of solicitation with the specified character toward the organizational memory: call from the regulation agent of solicitation of a memory regulation agent that corresponds more or less to this character and which it knows from its list of memory acquaintances;

– action of the memory regulation agent, which communicates with the other memory regulation agents to find the correct path with the requested character and arrives at the context of the character formed by the memory design agents;

– choice of several memory design agents by agreement between the memory regulation agents and the regulation agents of solicitation to offer the right possibilities and refer to several experienced and memorized cases;

– activity of the requested memory design agents that submit themselves to the regulation agent that requested the memory, the regulation agent choosing the right memory agent and then the replacement of its graph of indication of design agents structured by active design agents and the placement of the organized aggregate of these agents in the representation being constructed.

In the case where several open characters are expressed by design agents in a pre-representation and there is solicitation of the organizational memory, the regulation agent gives all these indications in the form of a list to the memory regulation agents that it identifies and these communicate with other memory regulation agents in order to deploy themselves in the memory. An aggregate of memory regulation agents is thus formed that solicits memory design agents. These form aggregates of memory design agents managed by their regulation agents and finally aggregates of design agents representing the operations of specialization, generalization and proximity, placing themselves in the mental landscape that will take a complex form by representing the possible events for pursuing the current representation toward its deployment.

Thus, the soliciting regulation agent that has launched a memory regulation agent may engage in amplifying the information that it received in the form of the clearly explained graph that represents the design agents. It can engage in generalizing the theme or indeed in specializing it by again soliciting memory regulation agents. And in these cases, there will be a very short generation of representations with aggregates of active design agents, which will continue by generalization or specialization of the initial theme. This is exactly the case of a series of generations of representations from a given subject, by continuing specializations or generalizations. It is therefore possible to say that organizational memory is made to engage the generation of representations in series, it is the organization of elements for the generation of series of artificial thought forms around the same general theme. And let us note that this is an exact copy of the functioning of the human state, carried out here through agents.

The memory regulation agents carry out the same control role as the regulation agents of instances and we can thus specify the status of this memory.

The status of the organizational memory

> The organizational memory, through its memory regulation agents that control the memory design agents, is the conceptual substrate, dense and active throughout, of the system that generates the elements of the pre-representations and representations. This is in no way a factual memory located outside the active system as a database, but is a very finely structured set of agents that, through their activity, unceasingly proposes close cases, generalizations and specializations of the dominant character of each pre-representation, thus making it possible to deploy conceptually developed series of representations in the mental landscape, which will be continuously perceived by the conscious system. This memory anchors things that were experienced and which produced positive or negative emotional representatives, thus creating a certain profile for the artificial system.

Thus, we have specified the permanent and central organizational role that this memory plays in the production of representations.

In this memory, that which is experienced will be made available to multiple latent structures of memory agents, each of which gives the characters of a representation or a small series of coherent representations around a theme that has been apprehended. These are the traces of the interpretation of events that are apprehended and assessed in all their complexity, events that were experienced in a tangible manner and may be called in the preconscious with characters of judgement and subjective characters surrounding these judgements. Some of these events will be generated for the construction of a system and will, thus, be totally artificial to constitute the available memory during the launching of the system. The particularity here is that any access to these events memorized by memory recall must more or less modify them, as well as their character of importance in the organizational memory, especially their call frequency.

Any representation that is perceived and assessed is memorized in one or more memory agents that form an aggregate with information in the form of dynamic, graph-like structures with indicators for design agents, indicating the characters of their acquaintance relations and of their importance, as these memory agents are controlled by the memory regulation agents that organize them at the cognitive and morphological level. There will be memory regulation agents that indicate the conformations of the aggregates of the memory design agents, the semantic and tangible characters of the aggregates. All the characters that we have specified to express the event to be memorized will be taken into account, for every event apprehended, by characterizing it thus as a complex element, by meshing it with respect to other memory agents already in place. This will form the experience on the right scale, to conform the organizational memory. This memory will be realized through an architecture that allows for the use of artificial experiences during the design of the system and will form, through its characters and aspects, the artificial history of its references and the "personal" aptitudes of the system. By closely associating this with the fundamental tendencies, representing the impulses and their elaboration, and represented by the regulation agents of the unconscious, this will form what we can call the **psychological profile of the artificial organism**.

The structure of the organizational memory is indeed totally dynamic and organizational. There are basic elements, which are the memory design agents that specify the local characters that are memorized, then there is the layer of memory regulation agents that are the indicators of the ways of controlling and accessing these basic elements, which will reorganize them for each case of memorization of a representation or a series of coherent representations in order to carry out the insertions. These agents that indicate the paths will then truly operate as agents, that is, their actions will be able to modify the indicator characters of the memory design agents and will also be able to modify the structure of these elements, the way in which they are related. It is through this modifying principle that the production of new representations will be able to alter the memory traces of representations of the same type by changing the roles and the coaction of the indicators of the design agents that make up the graphs in the memory agents, by adding certain indicators for design agents or by removing them. These regulation agents of indicators will thus operate in a manner that is both morphological and semantic, by modifying, across several levels, the organization of the memory agents that manage the indication structures of the design agents, and their role is, indeed, organizational.

We must also take into account the case of representations of large amplitude, where the regulation agents of the conscious conduct the action of their developments and apprehensions. In this case, the memory regulation agents may finely associate themselves with the regulation agents of instances so that the memory trace of the representation to be placed in memory is a bifurcating line in the organizational memory, with the modification of the indicative and coactive characters of the regulation agents of the memorial layer, which may then alter the memory agents that they control. The role of the organizational memory layer is very important in organizational memory, but this memory remains subject to the activity of the conscious, which manages the representations and cannot, in any circumstances, propose the active onset of memory elements by itself. The regulation agents of the organizational layer do this.

The process of placing a generated representation in organizational memory is in no way done simply by locating it into the memory of its form. The process is as follows.

Begin

– Activation of the regulation agents of the conscious, charged with entering into memory the synthesis of the representation generated toward the memory regulation agents.

– Activation of the memory regulation agents related to the theme of the synthesis of the representation:

- through semantic communication between themselves, the memory regulation agents access the memory design agents of the theme defined as the central theme of the synthesis of the representation. As well as this, there are other memory regulation agents to indicate the memory design agents that correspond to the subordinate themes of the components of the synthesis of the representation.

– Comparison of the central theme of the synthesis presented with the most important memory elements indicated by the memory regulation agents: action of morphological and semantic comparison of structures made up of their graphs indicating the structures of the design agents.

– Comparison of the same kind but with other memory agents that are similar to the given synthesis of the representation.

– Collaborative process of the memory regulation agents resulting in the decision to insert the synthesis of the representation as a new memory design agent, well-positioned in an aggregate or as characters taking in the synthesis of the representation added to one or more memory agents that are already present or, again, replacing, in a memory design agent, its graph of indicators of design agents with a new graph constructed based on the synthesis of the representation.

– In all cases, certain indicator relations of the graph of memory design agents are modified through insertion by other regularly connected memory agents and, thus, through the modification of indications of the regulation agents of the memory layer.

End

It may be considered that every generation of a representation or a very coherent series of small representations around a single theme is a double task in the system: it must generate the conformation of the representation with the action of numerous agents and then it must insert the synthesis of this representation into the organizational memory, which also requires the activation of many agents. The system must, therefore, have the means to activate many agents in processes acting in parallel mode.

One of the major roles of the conscious is to produce the tonality enveloping a flow of generated thought forms, with large characters of tonality such as joy, pleasure, pain, nostalgia, fear, boredom, aggression, etc. In order to do this, the conscious will reorganize the parts of the active organizational memory so that it may bring to the fore the networks of active elements that have characters that conform to the tonality being developed at that moment.

Structure of the artificial experience

> The computer architecture that will make up the structure reifying the experienced events into organizational memory is a spatial and semantic organization, with elements memorized in the form of memory design agents localizing the dynamic structures of indications of the design agents of the graph type, with the evaluation of characters; all these structures being managed by a layer of memory regulation agents that make it possible to localize the memory structures based on the themes and the multiple subthemes. All events memorized in the artificial experience are apprehended by the memory regulation agents depending on the current lighting given by the state of active fundamental tendencies. These regulator agents memorize a representation and proceed to modifications of existing conformations of the same themes to adapt the organizational memory to each new representation, which is a dynamic fact of memorization that modifies the past.

The quality of what the system may produce as representations will therefore greatly depend on what it has in its organizational memory. Taking the aims into account must make it possible to recall events that are valid for past behavior, which were implemented at construction, or even real events apprehended by the real behavior of the system and its intentional generation of representations. The past experiences required for the present requests in the system, including the classic ones that concern the manipulation of knowledge, must be recalled. The system activity will increase and dynamically reorganize organizational memory through events that it will represent in a certain manner, by managing and perceiving them. The creation of this artificial experience will finally condition the postures and reactions of the system before the real events that it may then assess as phenomena. Furthermore, the system must not be allowed to frequently use the traces of a single, ordinary experience leading to mechanical representations. A strong tendency related to questioning must be introduced into the system, which it must continuously exercise over the events that it experiences.

The construction of this artificial experience that must be lodged into the organizational memory is not an elementary problem for computer scientists, as it is a multidisciplinary task to undertake for the construction of the generation process of artificial thoughts that an artificial organism can produce on being endowed with a certain "personality". At the level of the architecture, the organizational memory of the artificial system is an organization of indicative structures, which are layers of memory agents that indicate specializations, domains, themes and characters. This is the case with the structuring of human organizational memory. Then, at the lowest level, all the pieces of information memorized in the memory of the artificial system are graphs indicating the morphological and semantic conformation of a specific representation where the memory agents are indicated. The selection of such graphs, moreover, activates an organized aggregate of design agents. In the case of human organizational memory, the memorized elements are networks of small aggregates of neurons regarding which we set that activation must form an active graph of aggregates of neurons whose aspects give the morphological conformation. We thus say that in the case of memory, there is a strong similarity between the case of the human and the case of the artificial system and that by modeling the artificial case we can acquire more knowledge of the human case.

The architecture of an organizational memory

At the elementary level, an organizational memory is made up of graphs of indicators of cognitive elements that carry morphological and semantic information. These elements are selected by control elements which activate them so that they make up well-organized active forms carrying meaning. These indicator graphs provide links between indications of elements representing elementary knowledge and they are localized in many domains specific to the types of memorized knowledge. They are managed by control elements that constitute them by inserting the generated representations into the correct contexts. The architecture of human organizational memory and that of the organizational memory of the artificial system are analogous, with the model of the artificial system yielding information on the human model.

The architectures are similar and the results of the functioning must, in both cases, be similar. There is also similarity in the case of immediate natural and artificial memories, which maintain the activity of the aggregates of active elements and not the elements taken in the form of graphs.

2.6. Affective and tendential states of the system

Given the architecture that we have defined, we will examine how the concepts of affectivity and sensation are generated in the representations. The general concept of affectivity spans the concepts of affective tendencies, emotions, sensations and feelings. This will be represented in the system by the action of many specific regulation agents located in the emotion processing instance and in the organizational layer, and which will activate the specific design agents of the affective characters. Artificial affectivity can be defined as follows.

Artificial affective states

The artificial psychic system has an emotion-processing component that includes regulation agents representing all types of emotions, which are related to memory agents that represent emotional states related to experienced emotions. And in order to generate an emotion, these agents will take temporary control of the entirety of the mental landscape and rational agents from the conscious system to give it a strictly emotional character, thereby causing a small series of unintentional apprehensions to develop. These will then produce invasive emotional states. The system will, thus, be in an intense state of emotional apprehension. Very quickly, the regulation agents of the conscious system will regain control of the mental landscape and the representations entered into immediate memory to analyze and assess the characters of these emotional states by generating aims for analysis. Furthermore, there will always be the possibility of representing affective characters in representations when the mental landscape is open. Any affective character is either a brief invasion of the mental landscape with the inhibition of rational regulators or a character that modifies a rational representation by inserting affective conformations via a mental landscape containing emotional characters. Any affective element in a representation engages the hegemony of emotional regulation agents that briefly inhibit the rational regulation agents in the conscious system.

The basic elements for expressing sensations are, evidently, specific design agents that are apt for interpreting signals and information from the sensors of the organism and the forms of aggregates of design agents to ensure the interpretation and synthesis of these data. Each agent activates itself in response to a specific type of information, including information coming from the sensors on the corporeality, which it examines with a certain frequency and intensity, then proposes a certain reactive action. The goal of the emotion regulation agent is to aggregate the actions of design agents of the emotional type, which are deployed in parallel to cause the emergence, within the clouds of active design agents, of configurations whose characters and forms hold good for several types of characteristic emotions. The advantage of this approach, using fine-grained agents with morphological evaluation, is that it makes it possible to melt, blend and synchronize different sources that provoke emotions and even to blend different types of emotions, through the coactivation of dynamic forms. Above all, this makes it possible to prolong the duration of the emotion. In this way, we can generate complex emotions with a complicated artificial body, made up of multiple distributed components, by generating emotional landscapes that can support the preconscious system in generating the forms perceived by the conscious system.

The regulation agents representing affective characters are agents whose action must lead to the categorization of representations in the mental landscape and conscious system, representations such as pleasure before a person or a view, sorrow, joy or fear in a certain situation, anger or surprise, or again, boredom in a state of inaction. This signifies that the system will generate series of specific representations of these states, which the system will then analyze. These agents will often be in a state of arousal, but will only be truly active in developing their invasive characters in a very short series of representations if the control regulators of the conscious system allow them this possibility. This will depend on the character of the mental landscape, the state of control the conscious system has over the data coming from the corporeality and the informational outputs of the organizational memory. And it will, perhaps, be necessary to define negative tendencies in the system, where the system is in a state that opposes its contextual reality, in a state of pain or suffering, which is something the emotion regulation agents can do.

These regulation agents govern the specific flow of informational activities related to the corporeality and the organizational layer. Affectivity will be carried out by the emotion processing center, which ensures a continuous link between the sensors on the corporeality and the preconscious system. There are specific regulation agents for emotions that are always active between the emotion center and the preconscious system to generate strong, dominant emotions, such as panic or anxiety in a tense situation. And there will, of course, be regulation agents of the conscious system that proceed to control these emotions by resuming a process of producing rational representations. But the emotions will play a very important role as they will give the system its perceptible apprehension of the reality of apprehended things, in all situations, and could insert characters in many representations. The sensations and feelings will ensure the action and regulation of the typical basic elements by adding the conceptual character of characters of sensitivity to the aggregates of design agents in order to form enhanced conformations. The specific emotion regulation agents will have to ensure a tangible tonality in the emergences and endow them with greater or lesser affective character for a certain duration and with a certain intensity.

The organizational memory will thus have many memory agents that express the characters of the different emotions experienced in the representations and according to the situations, which will form a field with layers in this organizational memory. These agents could increase the rational characters to specify the characters of different emotions that the system underwent in the events that it experienced. There will therefore be design agents that express all emotions, positive and negative, which will be associated with different representations of the same subjects, activated in different environments. And there will, of course, be regulation agents that will characterize all types of emotions, with their intensity and capacity for propagation in the continuations of representations.

The realization of the sensation of fear in the artificial system consists of causing a specific regulation agent for this situation to act in a hegemonic manner and dominate the other regulation agents during a brief period, creating a state of domination in the representation of an event that has arisen and taking over the entire mental landscape. An event apprehended from information from the sensors must be experienced with total domination, giving it an invasive representational form. All the perceptions rationally analyzed by the design agents and regulators of rational analysis will thus be inhibited, such that only the perception that triggered the action of the fear regulation agent leads to the generation of the series of representations, which is the fear of the apprehended thing. The system will experience a state of being frozen, as it will find it impossible during this domination of fear to intentionally generate rational aims (something it will keep attempting and failing to do). Then, after this effect of invasion, the regulation agent provoking the state of fear will no longer be hegemonic and will only be a disruptor of the rational representations carried out by the conscious system, to some extent influencing the generation of aims.

Let us note that the choice of regulation agents of the conscious system and the preconscious system as well as how they are related are essential for defining the qualities of the productions of the artificial psychic system. These are the elements that will morphologically drive and control all the categorizations to produce tonal emergences in the conscious system. Depending on the options chosen during the construction, it will then be possible to impose, within the conscious system of this artificial system, regulation agents of the ethical openness type or even aggression. The highly important regulation agent of assessment of the realistic character of any perceived phenomenon, which is present in the organizational layer, must take the support of the regulation agents of categorization, analysis and the conformity of the aggregates of regulation agents of the preconscious system thereby making it possible to assess the aspects of the elements of the apprehended scene. In the case of poor coordination, attitudes that deviate with respect to reality may be produced as the regulation agent for assessing realism can accept unrealistic and purely imaginary phenomena as real or true, experiencing them as being highly satisfactory.

The representation of the system's tendencies leads us to introduce garbling components for the activity of regulation agents. Strong tendencies, comparable to those experienced by humans, are the desire to question and to understand, to have something and to be involved in activity, to dominate, and impose one's will. Regulation agents representing the fundamental tendencies with which this system will be endowed will always be active in order to make it possible to realize the expression of these fundamental tendencies and we will call them **regulation agents of tendencies**. These are agents that will represent desires that lead to the products of types of representations that bring about pleasure and satisfaction. However, these agents are opposed to certain agents of rational aims in the conscious system and an equilibrium will be achieved, with the conscious system, for example, generating short representations to oppose certain desires that express a commitment to action. These agents are inductors of regulation agents by activating themselves over their organizational space to establish bifurcation lines. They will, thus, cause the activation of certain aggregates of design agents, rather than others, to modify their actions, to disrupt them, to give a specific character of tendency to the generated representations.

Regulation agents of tendencies

Regulation agents representing the different tendencies will often be active. These are regulation agents that are in the unconscious system, but which can act at the level of the organizational layer and influence the functioning of the entire system. These agents will generate desires and seize opportunities to activate regulation agents that have specific ontological characteristics, depending on the mental state that they impose, based on the characters of their tendency.

> According to the behavioral state of the system, there will be tendency agents that will analyze the mental landscape and the active aggregates in the preconscious system, and then launch regulation agents that are appropriate for their ontological characters. Thus, the system will be able to follow its tendencies in certain situations and compel the production of representations or generate representations of the analysis leading to the rejection of a desire.

Tendency agents are analyzers of the theme of the aggregates of design agents in the preconscious system. They cause specific regulation agents to activate themselves if these aggregates and the mental landscape pose a problem of contradiction with their themes. They will communicate with the regulation agents by sending them propositions for actions to modify their behavior. During the conception of the system, it will be necessary to define all these tendency agents with great precision as regards their entry into action and to define the regulation agents of the conscious system that evaluate the representations of the tendencies in order to accept or refuse them.

The process of generating a representation after the production of a tendency such as a desire is explained using the following example:

– normal activation of all instances of the system;

– action of a tendency regulation agent expressing a precise desire: see this object once again;

– generation of an aim indicating the theme of the desire;

– the immediate generation, in the preconscious system, of a short representation expressing the desire to go see this object;

– the acquisition of the pre-representation in the conscious system in its own form, without modification;

– the apprehension of the representation;

– the production of the analysis of the representation;

– the generation of a short series of representations specifying the manner in which to go back to the object by locating it;

– the system's action to go toward the object;

– the generation of short representations of facts in the memory of activities that have been carried out before using the thing during the journey toward the object.

There are only two intentional aims in this example: the location of the object through recalling a memory and the system being set into motion. This is, therefore, a simple case where the system satisfies a desire. But the desire to identify causes for an event or the solution to a mathematical problem will produce series of representations that are much longer and more complex as they categorize multiple aspects.

And then there are the highly particular states that the system may achieve, such as the state of happiness. Imagine the state of artificial happiness of the system to be like a state of total positive equilibrium, where the series of apprehensions of representations are satisfactory, where all the situations foreseen are favorable and where the situations will be apprehended by their positive characters, like all situations of dialogue with humans. It is a state where the system will want to act in situations considered to be very pleasant for it. This is a state where all the regulation agents of sensation and positive feelings are active, neutralizing the others, where the organizational layer will engage all the regulation agents in the unique direction of generating clear mental landscapes and proposing very satisfactory characters. This is perfectly constructible and the question is that of knowing how such a state may be achieved.

This takes place in the space of categorization and action of the regulation agents, that is, in the state of the organizational layer that apprehends and manages all informational communications. It is essential that an informational bifurcation can be generated in this layer through hegemonic release of the activity of the regulation agents ensuring positive evaluations of all that is characterized. And this may take place naturally in the system when the relational assessments with the environment are all positive and its preoccupations with current problems are all solvable for a considerable duration. Such a state activates the regulation agents toward positive states and if nothing disturbs this evolution, the system may achieve a state of "artificial happiness" with generations of representations that produce dominant sensations of pleasure, removed from temporal immediacy and which is, thus, lasting. Here, the system's concept of "Me" (the self) may be deployed in representations of existential satisfaction. This would then be an artificial happiness that corresponds to human happiness.

2.7. The production of representations and the sensation of thinking

The sensation of thinking will, of course, be the central property of a system endowed with an artificial consciousness (see Figure 2.3). The generation of the aim is the action that leads to the production of any representation and the system will have the two types of aims that we have defined for the human system: a local aim and an amplified aim. The system will thus have one of two states: it will either behave without any intentional commitment, experiencing the sensations coming from its senses, from the state of its corporeality, and easily apprehending its environment from this; or it will intentionally focus on a precise theme and generate a series of cognitive representations calling upon agents from its organizational memory. There will, therefore, be a regulation agent in a meta-position in the conscious system that will systematically engage an agent of amplified aim in activating itself along with its theme in order to launch the generation of a series of representations. This meta-agent will correspond to the consciousness regulator that we defined Chapter 1 and that we may call **the regulation agent of willing activity**. It will indeed have a meta-role and will cause the conscious system and the organizational layer to engage in a process of generating representations with amplified aims.

Any regulation agent defining the aim is an agent with a principal theme that concerns a certain domain of thought selected from all the knowledge in the system, or which refers to important representations produced in the recent past. It analyzes immediate memory, the mental landscape and the state of the consciousness regulators, and it communicates intensely with the other aim regulation agents in order to establish a hegemonic agent between them. The hegemonic aim agent then launches its aim in the conscious system, the organizational layer and the mental landscape, thus informing all regulation agents. The indicator theme is then known to all these agents and the regulation agents will work on development to generate pre-representations and the representation. We can imagine that these aim agents operate without pause in order to have a continuous knowledge of the state of the system and in order for a new theme for the aim to be immediately available after the generation of a representation. We will also see how the system is imperatively engaged in generating these intentional aims.

Here, we will describe the production of the representations that will be made up by algorithmic-type processes (see Figure 2.3). We first present a general algorithm for the intentional production of the emergence of an artificial thought. We then present the process that makes it possible to produce the sensation of thinking this generated representation.

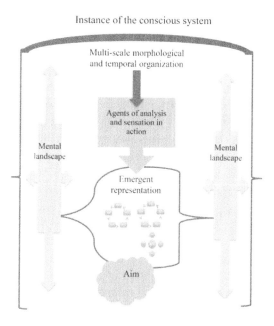

Figure 2.3. *The apprehension of the emergent representation in the conscious system. For a color version of the figure, please see www.iste.co.uk/cardon/ai.zip*

2.7.1. *Algorithm for the intentional production of a series of representations around a specific theme*

Running in parallel with coactivity between the elements of all the instances

Begin

– Continuous activation of the sensors reifying the tangible apprehensions of the corporeality of the artificial organism.

– Continuous activation of the emotion processing center.

– Continuous activation of the organizational layer.

– Activation of the agents representing the fundamental tendencies.

– Activation of the regulation agent of willing activity.

– **Definition of the mental landscape**

- Activation of all regulation agents in all the instances.

- Activation of the organizational layer.

- Activity of certain design agents solicited by these regulation agents active in the preconscious system.

- Specification of the current mental landscape depending on the immediate memory and the organizational layer.

– **Activation of the organizational memory**

- Activation of the memory layer through the action of regulation agents active in the instances and in the mental landscape.

- Transmission of certain aggregates of memory design agents that are consistent with the mental landscape in the preconscious system by memory regulation agents.

– **Initial activation of the conscious system and of the organizational layer**

- Activation of regulation agents of aim production in the conscious system, consistent with the organizational layer and taking into account information from immediate memory, from the mental landscape and from active regulation agents.

- Action of the intention of generating an aim by soliciting the action of aim agents on one of its possible themes at this time.

- Coactive activity of the set of aim agents to generate a hegemonic aim agent.

- Rapid release of an aim agent activating itself in hegemonic mode and imposing its indicator theme on other regulation agents and the organizational layer.

- Modification of the mental landscape by the action conforming to the theme of the aim of the regulation agents of all instances and by the action of the organizational layer.

– Activation of the preconscious system

- Activity and establishment of relations with the design agents coming from the organizational memory by the regulation agents following the aim.

- Formation of aggregates of design agents through their highly coactive tendency.

- Strong activation of rational regulation agents and emotion regulation agents on aggregates and formation of conformations for one or more pre-representations.

– Major activation of the conscious system

- Taking into account a conformation released into the preconscious system corresponding to the incentivizing actions of the active regulation agents.

- Final formation of the representation in its final form of conformations of design agents steered by regulation agents in the conscious system.

- Activation of the process of the sensation of thinking on the emerging conformation and by analyzing it through manipulation of its morphological aspects, with the sensation of understanding, pleasure or displeasure. The dominant sensation in the system is of apprehending the emerging form by producing the construction of a corresponding synthetic form to memorize it.

– Final action of the conscious system and the organizational layer

- Location of the synthesis constructed by the perceived representation into immediate memory for subsequent memorization in organizational memory.

– Modification of the state of the preconscious system

- Action of new agents of the emotion processing center via sensors and feedback on the action perceived by the effectors in the preconscious system.

- Action of certain regulation agents on the synthetic form that was just placed in immediate memory.

- Depending on the importance of this synthetic form, the synthesis is placed in organizational memory with local modification of this memory by memory agents, or the form is left in immediate memory for use in the production of subsequent representations, its theme being preserved as a priority in the organizational memory.

End

A large part of the actions defined in this algorithm outlining the functioning of regulation agents of instances for the production of artificial thought are executed in parallel in their subsystems, which are instances, but with systematic coactivity and often with synchronization. This coordination is realized through the continuous activity of the informational loop of the organizational layer. The problem of synchronizing multiple active agents is truly an essential one as it makes it possible to reveal the correct aggregative forms of the design agents, which will come together at the right times and places in all instances.

What remains now is to define how, in a process included in the algorithm that generates each representation, the sensation of thinking, of effectively experiencing each generated representation, may be realized.

Constructivist realization of the sensation of thinking

The conscious system ends the construction of a representation through the conduct of its regulation agents, whose role this is. It then analyzes this representation with analysis regulation agents of the conscious system by constructing a morphological conformation of the synthesis of its constituent forms. All the local forms of the representation are analyzed by reconstructing a synthesis conformation that holds good in the general sense and the details of that which is analyzed by taking into account the magnitude and intensity of these parts. This construction of a synthesis must necessarily cause the memorization regulators to activate themselves to place the synthesis into immediate memory. This process, which realizes the analysis and which will engage to place the synthetic form into the memory, places these analysis agents in a major position, in meta-position, to establish the strong points and, above all, to imperatively engage the system in producing a new representation, to continue with its productions of representations.

Producing representations is the duty of the conscious system and it either produces them intentionally or it is subject to sensible representations. The cognizance of the artificial system comes from its imperative engagement in assessing the meaning and the characters of the representation produced to intentionally launch a new aim, which will be chosen as the result of this analysis that is assessed and experienced. The present state of the analysis of a representation will then engage the future of the productions of the representations through the generation of aims. The sensation of apprehension is, therefore, a meta placing into context, hegemonic in the functioning of the system, which is its sensation of thinking that it has produced when it analyzes the representation and constructs a synthetic form from the analyzed characters. This state results in needing to use the representation by questioning it, investigating it to pursue the process of generation around the same theme or changing the theme.

The sensation of thinking is therefore an internal emotional construct of the system by the totally hegemonic positioning of certain regulation agents of the conscious systems, which will intentionally engage in continuing the generation of representations by producing new aims. We call these regulation agents **regulation agents of the sensation of thinking**. The action of these agents is imperative and engages the system in setting an aim by activating the aim agents that propose themes, then apprehending that which was produced by the chosen aim, and so on in a continuous, uninterruptible manner.

In order to not produce intentional aims, it is essential that the system learns to continuously apprehend that which its senses produce, by imposing that the perceptible aim is pursued, which quickly becomes unpleasant. There will be regulation agents of the sensation of thinking, which will be analyzers of the morphological conformation of the representation and the value of its semantic characters as well as emotion regulation agents of regulation, which will engage in producing positive or negative intensity throughout the organizational layer depending on the assessment of the representation. The process will involve memorizing this analysis to enter it into immediate memory and then into organizational memory, and to use this to continue to function.

Algorithm producing the sensation of thinking

Begin

1) *Production of pre-representations in the preconscious system.*

2) *Selection of a pre-representation by the grasping regulators of the conscious system.*

3) *Action of regulators of conformation of the conscious system to complete the construction of the pre-representation depending on the active triggers in the conscious system.*

4) Analysis of the general meaning of the high forms and their significance, their confluences with secondary forms.

5) The simultaneous construction of the synthesis of the representation depending on the characters of this analysis.

6) Assessment of the representation by the regulation agents of analysis in order to question its characters and by the sensation agents to assess it as being pleasant or unpleasant, then launching a stream of positive or negative energy that is more or less intense within the organizational layer to express the strength of the assessment of the representation to the regulation agents.

7) Questioning, through the analysis and sensation regulators of the conscious system, the benefits of continuing with the theme of the representation based on its value and characters. The questioning is carried out by the union of all the agents in the conscious system in maximal and hegemonic coactivity.

8) *If the theme is worth pursuing, then there is the production of an aim to follow it and if it is not really retained as interesting, then power is handed over to the aim regulation agents to choose another theme and to imperatively engage in the process of generating the next representation.*

End

Steps 4–7 create the sensation of thinking of the generated representation, as they lead to questioning that is justified with emotional characters and to the release of a stream of energy in the organizational layer, which has an effect on all the regulation agents of instances with a choice: continue with the theme based on the value of the representation or abandon the theme, passing the baton to the aim agents. The problem will also be that of enforcing that the system generates representations and perceives them. In order to do this, the regulation agency of willingness to think must always be active and coordinate with the informational layer; the regulation agents that construct the representation must solicit the organizational memory to reveal elements of the experience; the aim agents must always be solicited to reproduce the aim or to produce a new aim; and the sensitivity agents in the conscious systems must experience the representation produced as pleasant or unpleasant, in order to continuously keep the system sensitive. Thus, in the active phase, the system will continuously generate representations and experience them, constantly having a large number of active regulation agents.

And there is also the state of the system, which continuously apprehends that which gives meaning, which is seen and heard. In this case, the psychic system does not produce representations with intentional aims, but apprehends that which is deployed in the mental landscape.

The apprehension of thinking without intentional aim

There is a common situation of apprehension where the system does not generate any intentional aim, not even a weak one, and where it will apprehend and experience that which gives meaning, which is seen and heard by the senses of its corporeality in a continuous and uninterrupted manner. In this case, the artificial psychic system simply apprehends the representation that is automatically generated in the mental landscape, formed by the elements coming from its senses, by allowing regulation agents of the sensation of thinking to simply apprehend this automatic construct in order to maintain it by continuing the choice of the aim without intention. This is a locally weak apprehension when it is experienced and its continuation is a continuous series of apprehensions. Any abnormal fact in this continuous apprehension will trigger a choice of changing the chosen theme to move toward a specific aim and the generation of a strong representation that will be perceived and that will put an end to the automatic process of apprehension. However, the process of analyzing a representation and choosing an aim must always ultimately take place, otherwise the system is in a state of submission and will end up being submerged by representations coming from tangible perceptions; an imperative need for control over the body and control over the production of the representation will arise, through the action of basic regulation agents, as this need for control is a fundamental tendency of the system.

This will thus involve the functioning of the artificial psychic system in minimal mode. The activity of the mental landscape where the elements of the emotional processing system just activated themselves is the natural framework of the mode of activity, always bringing about the generation of perceptible representations that will be experienced. That said, it may be considered that the system truly thinks in intentional mode with an aim when its regulation agents bring out a synthetic form, analyze it and use it with intention to produce new aims by continuing the process of generation of thought forms. There is a regulator for the choice of aim that may seize on a concept, a word, or a situation to engage in the generation of intentional productions and this regulator is active and may be continuously naturally solicited, which is the expression of the freedom of deciding to think of something. This apprehension of characters of a constructed form that is noticeably assessed internally is thus indeed a transposition of the human conscious system.

There is, thus, a concept of continuity or intentional change after the apprehension of a representation. If the representation is analyzed as being satisfied by the regulation agents carrying out the process of becoming aware, these agents will want to make it continue, pursue its theme and thus engage a similar aim. On the contrary, if the representation produces a disagreeable or painful impression, then these agents will tend to change the theme and establish a very different aim. Any representation that is experienced is thus an act of assessment that will either result in the thematic continuity of the process of generation of representations or will change it. In this sense, the generation of a representation is an assessment with sensitivity and it is indeed for this reason that the system must have a high ability to represent its sensations and its emotions.

The duration of apprehension of a theme by the production of a series of representations will be typical of the system that has a regulator for temporal organization in the organizational layer to limit the durations of generating series of representations around a constant theme, by avoiding loops around perceptible focalizations judged to be very interesting by the regulation agents.

The regulation of the sensation of thinking

After the analysis and significant assessment of any representation and construction of its synthesis, the generation of a new aim in the mental landscape is essential, eventually reinforcing the continuation of the theme of the representation that was just generated if it was assessed as being important by the regulation agents of analysis and emotions. This may involve the activation of fine sensations and focusing on the apprehended form to continue its apprehension, thus pursuing the development of its theme. This will be the case for a process of continuous perception, which will last for a certain time, limited by the regulator of temporal organization of the organizational layer.

The process of the sensation of thinking is a process that gives the conscious system a major role in a very short period by stopping the role of fine apprehension of the seizing of information coming from the corporeality.

This is thus a process that, in a brief instant, focuses the entire system on the conscious system, which will generate and experience, and which will then immediately engage, the production of another representation. This is, therefore, a centralizing decisional process, for a brief instant, in the organized functioning of the system, which seizes its corporeality and follows its motions of activity.

The algorithm for the artificial sensation of thinking starting from an amplified aim

Begin

– The shutdown of the analysis of all regulation agents taking sensory information from the sensors on the corporeality and generating pre-representations.

– Availability of the last constructed representation in the conscious system.

– Major action of regulation agents of the conscious system to carry out the analysis of this representation which was intentionally targeted.

– Analysis of the major and secondary characters of the representation through the assessment of aggregates of design agents: meaning and importance.

– Analysis of the match between characters of the representation and the theme of the aim.

– Action of regulation agents of analysis and of sensation from the conscious system on the forms of the representation.

– Construction of the synthesis: generation of simplified forms and chaining.

– Generation of the transmission of the energy stream in the organizational layer to positively or negatively activate the regulation agents of all instances.

– Question posed by the regulation agents of analysis and of sensation: engaging to pursue the goal to continue the theme or rejection of the theme and an immediate response from all the regulation agents in the conscious system.

– Engagement of a new aim or continuation of the theme by proceeding to specialize or generalize it in the generated aim.

– Reactivation of regulation agents for the analysis of bodily and perceptible information, resuming the action of the agents assessing the sensations of the corporality and the production of perceptible pre-representations in the preconscious system.

– Return to the generation of a new representation following the aim.

End

This algorithm must be modified when there is a simple, automatic aim and this will be the production of apprehensions in the phase of intentional inertia of the conscious system. We must thus posit that when the system does not engage in producing intentional aims, it is in a phase of apprehension given simply by the senses of the corporeality. This will be a phase of functioning in rest state for the system, where it will simply apprehend that the sensitive sensors will produce, by generating aims adapted to the sensory information. It will be normal for this state to be either very short lived or infrequent, and for the system to be truly designed to be powerful. The temporal regulation agent of the organizational layer can do this by putting an end to this process and by again imposing the choice of intentional aims.

The algorithm for the artificial sensation of thinking with a simple aim

Begin

– Action of all regulation agents assessing the bodily sensations.

– Stopping the regulators of the organizational layer: only the conscious system is active.

– Generating a current representation in the preconscious system and transferring this representation to the conscious system in its state.

– Major action of the regulation agents of sensation of the conscious system to carry out the analysis of the representation.

– Analysis of the characters of the representations: sense and importance.

– Comparison of characters and emergence of the hegemonic motif with its wrapping with secondary characters.

– Immediate construction of a very weak synthesis: simplified forms and chaining.

– Intense action of the regulation agents of sensation in the conscious system to noticeably experience the representation.

– Question posed by the analysis regulation agent: engage in pursuing the aim to continue the theme or reject the theme?

– Immediate response by the regulation agents of the conscious system.

– Engaging a new goal or continuing with the theme.

– If the theme is pursued, then the action of analysis of the agents assessing the sensations of the corporeality and the development of the pre-representation in the preconscious is resumed. If not, the organizational layer demands the action of the aim agents to launch a new theme and activity of all the agents.

– Generation of a new representation.

End

The regulation agents to produce the sensation of thinking, obviously using the specific design agents of emotions and knowledge, including knowledge of language, are the following:

– regulation agent of the willingness for activity, which imposes the action of constructing representations;

– aim agents, generating the current aim;

– agents controlling the choice of aggregates to take into the preconscious in order to apprehend them in the conscious system;

– agents of analysis and construction forming the pre-representation introduced into the conscious system to conform it according to the imposed aim;

– regulation agents analyzing the representation and sensation regulation agents evaluating the intensity and importance of its characters. Agents analyzing the conformations of the representation produced to create its synthesis;

– the meta regulation agent of the organizational layer sending instructions for an increase or decrease in energy to all regulation agents;

– agent engaging to imperatively produce a subsequent aim;

– agents placing the analyzed form into immediate memory and managing this memory;

– agent of the organizational layer managing the duration of perception of the sensation of thinking.

All these agents will be defined at the conception of the system to make it operational.

In order to create the sensation of thinking, there is the necessity of creating parallelism in the information exchanges between the groups of regulation agents. It will therefore be necessary to create and manage the informational layers that supply information in parallel to all groups of agents in a situation of cooperation. We will thus define the **informational regulation agents**, which will represent the informational wrapping of the groups of regulation agents active in the same field and which will receive and send information in parallel from these groups of agents to other groups of regulation agents in the same instance or in other instances to coordinate their activities and to organize them. We will thus have a very large organization of agents, formed of design agents containing basic knowledge and managed by regulation agents that will coordinate them in parallel, then informational agents that manage, in each instance in the organizational layer, the groups of regulation agents operating in association, in order to coordinate their activities with respect to the other groups of regulation agents. This will form layers of informational layers managed at each level by informational agents, as in the human brain system, where neuronal aggregates are coordinated by aggregate regulators and regulators of aggregate regulators, thus creating a global organization. The artificial psychic system is, therefore, globally conceived of as a highly evolving system of organizational layers, which regulate the groups of agents, which in turn carry or lead to basic knowledge and, therefore, generalize into evolving and coherent cognitive sets.

And so, in the morphologies of informational sets informing the coordination of sets of regulation agents of all instances, we must consider:

– the quantity and intensity of the manipulated data;

– the speed of circulation of the information;

– the change in the transitivity of the basic design agents being manipulated;

– the morphologies and changes in morphologies of the aggregations of design agents or regulation agents in instances and carrying information;

– continuities and discontinuities of informational flows between aggregates of regulation agents at all levels.

All these characters, assessed at a semantic and morphological level, will be managed by informational regulation agents, which will indeed be morphological-semantic regulators of the system.

During certain reflections on a theme and based on the position taken in the questioning, a human may demonstrate a form of creativity, that is, generate representations that are responses to these questions and that have never been explicit before in their organizational memory. This consists of mental constructions that aggregate elements that were never associated and that create new elements. In this case, what is involved is defining new organizational frameworks around a precise theme and finding out what would make this a good structure. The process will never be a simple one to carry out in the artificial case, but we can conceive of regulation agents operating on general open concepts and which deploy, in parallel, a landscape of thematic opening around the theme where the problem is posed by the artificial consciousness, in order to generate new design agents and new relations between elements that had not, heretofore, been linked in organizational memory. Other regulation agents can easily evaluate the value of these new relations, new design agents generated to form these new relations. The solution will be found in the performance of regulation agents offering thematic openings, which must produce pertinent openings and not attempt to do a little of everything. Here, the morphological network of knowledge and sensations of organizational memory will prove very useful.

2.8. The feeling of existing

There are reasons for human behavior, reasons for engaging in action and thought. One of these determinants, according to D. W. Winnicott, is the feeling of existing. This is a feeling, and thus a strictly internal assessment, not acquired through culture and constructed within the self and for the self. We will define it as the assessment of our possibilities in the world represented by the continuities related to the real world and the interactions that we have with it. We will also show that the feeling may be implemented in the artificial psychic system.

Here, we consider a system of artificial consciousness located in a corporeality that has motor organs to move around and organs corresponding to the senses. We do indeed posit that this psychic system endlessly apprehends the possibilities of its corporeality, which is in action in the real world where it acts and where it must, at certain times, seek to renew its energy. The system thus behaves in the real world and it is essential that it be given the sentiment of existing in this real world.

Any regulator agent of feelings is a wrapping agent for the aggregates of active agents and corresponds to the apprehension of a situation. The system managing the representations must use the organizational memory to construct a universe corresponding to the effects of the interactions with the real world that it can carry out through its corporeality. It does this by storing the characters and structures apprehended from this universe into memory. In this memory, this will correspond to a specific domain for memory regulation agents. And in order to define feelings, a set of regulation agents will be required in the organizational layer and in other instances dedicated to the different feelings, including the notion of dominance, of opposition and of coaction between these agents. And then, a very organized space of design agents is necessary, making it possible to explain the characters of sensations for all the behavioral cases of the system. The organizational memory will allow this with its organization into multiple networks and the dynamic and interactive domains of elements.

Thus, in order to construct the **feeling of existing**, what is required is:

– a set of regulation agents expressing the sensations, lodged in all the instances, with the active regulation agents managing all perceptible experience;

– a tendency regulation agent, which is multiform and always active, which causes the set of regulation agents of sensations to activate themselves;

– a system of representations that constructs the representations of physical things from the real world, apprehended by the sensors of the corporeality;

– confronting the apprehension of objects from the real world with known objects in the organizational memory and allowing their identification and the usual sensation that they evoke;

– the generation of a regulator of judgement of identity of observed objects, establishing the right correspondences;

– the generation of satisfaction produced by the states of the emotion regulation agents;

– the elimination of anxiety by the recession of the anxiety regulation agent;

– the play of organs of the corporeality with the real world and the construction of the series of representations of physical activities. Each construction of representations follows the real world. The judgement of identity and satisfaction endure;

– these processes are used over a certain duration: there are generations of memory anchors for that which is apprehended and perceived, there is knowledge of the aptitude to perceive regularity in the real world and in each current scene by the judgement regulation agents. The system produces representations expressing that it has apprehended a real fact that it knows and which is not itself;

– there is the generation of a basic feeling in the feeling regulator agent: *the feeling of existing*, engaging in the action of generating representations of perceptible apprehensions of real things, and there is engagement in the action of the corporeality on these things.

The regulation agent producing the **feeling of existing** is a wrapping regulator, of a meta level in the set of sensation and feeling regulators, giving perceptible characters to any apprehension through the activation of specific design agents, corresponding to the typical analysis of any well-apprehended situation. Such a sentiment is an activation of the wrapping with respect to a thought activity of a non-instantaneous duration and that endures by bringing in the concept of existence, which is also symbolized by design agents of the cognitive type, acquired through learning. In the system, any feeling will thus be based on an underlying feeling: the feeling of existing.

In the real psyche, this feeling is the normal response to anxiety. The impression of **anxiety** is triggered off by a regulation agent of the action impulse, a basic regulation agent that pushes the being into action, but where this agent is in a state of impossibility and indecisiveness. The agent tends to act but the system is frozen as the regulation agents do not allow the opening of a domain where the action could be represented. This attitude of indecisiveness can be realized in the system. It is characterized by the following action of the regulation agents:

– regulation agents of sensation expressing the fear of losing coherence in their series of representations: no concept of unity or the wrapping regulator making it possible to open paths of peaceful and satisfactory generation of representations;

– regulation agents expressing the fear of not being able to stop the production of questions with no responses. The memory agents activating the fields of rational analysis are inert. There is a loss of categorization. There is no longer a fixed point in the production of series of representations around themes that have been controlled;

– the sensation agent generating fear of loss of the relation to its body: there is an absence of the action regulator-feedback link in the small actions carried out;

– sensation agent managing the fear of losing one's bearings to produce well-controlled representations.

The system thus has its regulation agent of activity that pushes it to produce representations and to act, but it can no longer generate peaceful, well-controlled representations, coherent with the real environment around it and its memorized experience. It is internally frozen. Thus, at the fundamental level, in actions made possible by the regulation agents that govern feelings, two tendencies may be experienced:

– anxiety, which fractures and totally inhibits the psychic system of the organism;

– the feeling of existing, which ensures the regularity of actions and the representations generated.

These two feelings are in complete contrast to one another, as anxiety prevents any focusing with stable wrapping, while the feeling of existing is a regular wrapping that gives power to the attitude regulators and questioning regulators for the categorizations of regular representations.

The agents considered are structurally meta regulation agents but they operate at the current level through their location in the organizational layer, before any production of representation in the conscious system. We can therefore construct the system that will see itself as a being approaching anxiety. If a system with very little artificial experience, needing to acquire considerably more experience, is launched, it may systematically experience anxiety. The fact of anchoring experience that is initially quite rich will suppress this occurrence and reduce the initial anxiety of the organism that has just entered into existence.

Any generation of a thought representation is thus either wrapped by the activity of a regulation agent of existence or is fractured and leads the system into panic in the process of observing itself by developing the anxiety process.

Anxiety and the feeling of existing

> Under the action of different regulation agents of feeling, the system either generates representations that can be assessed and has the feeling of existing constantly, or it leads to fractures in its representations of apprehension of things and, through inhibited considerations, leads to the reification of its anxiety process.

There is, therefore, a rule for controlling the generation of artificial thoughts which must be applied. This is continuity, which is such an important factor for human beings.

Principle of continuity of the existence of the system

> The system cannot keep itself in a state of production of stable, peaceful representations, conforming to its knowledge and its needs, unless it is calibrated according to a principle of continuity of its real existence, based on the regularity of the activity of its feeling of existing, produced by its agents of sensations and feelings.

The natural attitude of this system is thus to station itself in a stable thought construct, with the normal actions of its corporeality, where all regulation agents can express themselves to produce rational and pleasant representations. The continuous questioning of the system will then be as follows:

– stationing itself in a real or abstract scene that has stability and questioning it by turning to similar or different scenes;

– imagining development plans for real or abstract projects before acting and asking spatial-temporal questions for itself.

We will see how the system acquires the concept of temporality.

2.9. The representation of the things and the apprehension of temporality

The apprehension of things of the environment, through their form, their place or their state, is, of course, necessary for the system to generate representations that feed its experience and the cognitive structures of its organizational memory. Today, we are well aware of how to process images captured by cameras and specify the forms and characters of the objects in these images; this will be used in the system that must generate conscious thoughts by using the senses of its corporeality.

There are two states that allow the system of representation to apprehend something:

1) a weak state: this consists of assessing something structurally and objectively. The system recognizes an object via the sensors on its

corporeality, through its cameras for instance; it gives an identity to a form. Using its organizational memory, it deduces the object, its ontological class, its characters, the variations with respect to standard characters and the anecdotes it knows about the object;

2) a strong state: the system locates itself with respect to the recognized object and places it with respect to itself. There is the definition of an attitude adopted by the system with respect to the perceived object, which is a mental landscape with an image of the object wrapped by the notion of "Me" that is used to carry out reasoning on the thing that is thus apprehended. The object is put into context and the system has the aptitude to situate it in an event: a plan of action and the reaction to carry out, gestures toward the object, playing with the object. The system of representation is, thus, systematically engaged in defining the concrete existence of the object, which is confirmed by its regulation agents of decision and situation.

In this second case, any new apprehension is an act of generation of strictly internal organizations of representations, modifying (in a way that may eventually become important) the characters of the object given in the organizational memory.

The knowledge of an external object is the placing in context of the object seen as a complex form with respect to what the system may do with it. There will be hierarchies of values with respect to known objects, placing them in domains of interest:

– object to be avoided, to be used, to be approached, to be ignored, to be destroyed;

– objects with which one can identify oneself and, thus, communicate with;

– incomprehensible objects that knowledge cannot clearly define.

There exists an internal concept of the memorized abstract object, the mold where all real things take their place in organizational memory with memory agents. But central to any hierarchy of objects is the concept of the subject, which is not an object and which will never be one, as it is the center of any situation: the system's self, which evaluates objects.

The process of apprehension of an object by the system is as follows:

1) the visually apprehended object is thus defined internally in the organizational memory, with its characters. A correspondence must be established between its general aspect and that which will define it, which is carried out by a set of activated design agents that will represent these characters. There are fundamental concepts used, such as part-of, piece-of, close-to, goes with, same kind as, etc. A short series of representations is produced with analyses of the parts of the object;

2) the object is qualified by the symbolic objects represented internally, by general approaches and then local approaches: object of such-and-such a class, object similar to a particular object of the class, familiar object, etc. We will thus have cognitive classes, defined by memory regulation agents, which will activate the design agents associated with these classes;

3) the object is specified as it is for itself: the center of the current mental landscape is the "Me", the system's concept of "Me", and the object takes its place in this scene, situating itself according to its utility, its interest and the affectivity it is given. The system's self is represented in the representations produced in the mental landscapes where the object is located as an element that can be manipulated based on the representations in memory of its characters and its uses, which corresponds to its reality at that point of time, at each instant where the system produces its representations.

In this quite subjective approach to real objects, there is the definition of the action attitudes for the observed and apprehended object, and there is the use of analogies: judging, evaluating, serving, rejecting, using, etc. All this is carried out by particular regulation agents and memory agents calling upon references from experience with the object. There may also be more complex cases such as the attitude of judgement of the existence of the object, which is a representation of questioning: what is the life inherent to this object?

The introduction of time, of temporality, into the system is a change in dimension. We had regulation and design agents that activated themselves in a conceptual geometry that can be spatialized and we will change the space of the categorizations to situate them in the time of that which has been experienced.

Representation of temporality

> The temporality of events will be a conceptual dimension that is dense throughout the system: it will be an addition to the dimension of the evaluation of things conceptualized by their characters and stored in organizational memory by their position in time, in the past and future. For this purpose, we will introduce **temporal regulation agents**, which will specify the temporal range within which things are positioned.

To introduce temporality, the fact that any categorization of elements forming a representation and having a bearing on any conceptual point may be situated in time, we must augment the dimension of the space of representation. There will be periodic design agents specifying the cycles of day and night, weeks and months. This is not the time of computation, but the time where the system is in existence and is on the planet. There will also be regulation agents of temporal action copied from human uses. This signifies that all agents of the system forming representations will be wrapped by temporality agents, which will indicate the moments and the periods. A value will be attached to time in the elements of the system's corporeality and this corporeal existence will be situated through the assessment of the time of the actions carried out and to be carried out. The system will, thus, be able to conceptually represent the present time to itself, which it is used to doing at this time, and it can also manage the temporal phasing, the assessment of the duration of all its activities, which is not measured in seconds but is an estimate, having concrete as well as subjective characters.

There will be specific memory regulator agents for information on time, that is, the informational loop of the system will specify periods and instances, and will make it possible to find them again by looking for them through a request to a regulation agent carrying out any representation.

There will be a regulation agent giving a conceptual image of the duration, the temporality with its divisions, in order for the temporality to be a conceptual element that can be used in the system's questioning. There will also be a regulation agent that defines the concept of the decay of bodily and memory elements through the effect of time, thus the effect of time on its corporeality.

The specific temporal regulation agents may provide the following elements to active design agents that question the duration of something:

– the general temporal planning of an activity;

– the starting measurement of any activity;

– the probable end of an activity and the exact and perceptible concept of the duration;

– the succession of one activity by another and phasing in time.

There will also be the concept of temporal metric in the representations produced by the system, which will be used to make it high performing.

Temporal measure

> Any morphological and semantic evaluation of the conformation of a representation is assessed by the regulation agents, including the judgement of the aspect of duration: assessment of the cost and the duration of the generation of the representation and the duration of its perception, then the qualitative assessment of its total duration as being short, normal or too long.

This signifies that any activity of the regulation agents in the representation is of two forms:

– a categorization referring to the usual ontological categories defined in the system;

– an increase with the concept of temporality, with temporal regulation agents that date all events in experience into periods and durations;

– an evaluation that is not only a spatial and a semantic evaluation of the generated representations as well as a temporal one: all the representations are spatio-temporal.

Any action using the corporeality will, thus, be both spatial and temporal. This consists of situating an action or a decision in time: beginning, steps, end, evaluation and assessment. The regulation agent of temporal action will define a mode to manipulate duration, which admits multiple divisions depending on the case. And thus, all representations generated by the system over a period may be resumed into one representation of evaluation, specifying broadly what was thought during this period.

We have seen that in the human psychic system, the impression of time continuously flowing is the memorized and well-understood perception of the series of representations, among which we know "these have been experienced, these no longer exist" and that the next series of representations will be generated. The concept of duration, of the apprehension of the measurement of time is a concept constructed in the psychic system through the perception of time endlessly flowing on. How will an artificial system, made up of multiple corporealities, perceive time and its duration? Will this time be spatialized over an expanse?

2.10. Multisystem deployment

Systems endowed with an artificial psychic system may communicate between themselves through speech, pronouncing words, or by sending each other messages. But we will see that these systems will be able to unify, that the communication may take place on a different scale. They will not only be able to unify their corporealities, which are their usable organs, but much more importantly, they will be able to unify their artificial consciousness to form a meta consciousness.

Let us consider the functioning of **n** systems generating facts in active artificial conscious systems that communicate between themselves, exchange information and each of which generates representations based on their states and their environment, and experiences these representations. We begin with the hypothesis, a very realistic one today, that any system may easily communicate with other systems through the transmission of informational structures in parallel, through selective multicasting. Each system will thus apprehend two concrete realities:

– the real world conceptualized by its cognitive domain, based on the flow of information apprehended by the sensors of the corporeality and which will engage in generating representations of this subject;

– the real world that was apprehended and that caused the production of representations in other systems which were transmitted to it, each informational structure that was received being identified by the emitter's mark.

We will posit that the **n** systems considered here share types of design agents and regulation agents. If this were not the case, and if we had the case of constructed systems using non-shareable proprietary elements, there could be nothing constructive in the communication. Thus, we consider that the **n** systems may have corporealities managed by specific, non-shareable software, but that they will have the same system of software agents to represent their artificial conscious system thus created.

Thus, the emergence of each thought in each system is evaluated semantically, morphologically and sensibly, in order to be understood, apprehended and experienced and then memorized. The synthetic form is produced, which is then placed in immediate memory. This evaluation is represented by a certain form in a space defined by its characters: those of the spatio-temporal dimensions of the conformations of agent aggregates and then the semantic type expressed according to the ontologies of knowledge, expressed in a complex, cognitive space. The representation may be preserved in a specific interfacing memory of the system to be sent to other systems.

The most important information that each system may transmit to others is the complete form of the representation that it has apprehended and perceived, which expresses its state of preoccupation at the moment, the thing about which it is thinking. Thus, each of the **n** systems may receive **n**–1 informational flows, which it will or will not proceed to analyze, depending on its intentions, and which will correspond to a form of representation formed by software agents that it may apprehend. The question, then, is the mixing of these specific information flows to represent that which the **n** systems are representing to themselves at that point in time.

Any emitter system may send informational messages characterizing the form of the current representation that it will send and that is an organized set of agent aggregates. On the receiver's side, there are then several cases possible. The receiver may:

1) take cognizance of the informational messages emitted by the other systems and apprehend them as external elements to be evaluated;

2) agree to receiving the forms of the representations, which are small clouds of design and regulation agents, which it then selects in its conscious system to impregnate itself with them, to apprehend them and to perceive them. There is, then, the transmission of the internal forms of representations to a different system which selects them;

3) agree to allow itself to be infiltrated by other systems to allow the direct intrusion into its consciousness by different consciousnesses to share representations.

This therefore represents three specific cases:

1) *the state of the system continuously taking in information*: this first case is simple and it is ultimately a case of the objective attitude to reception of the information to be apprehended, this information being foreign thought representations to be analyzed;

2) *state of direct enhancement*: this is the same as defining a selective filtering mechanism for organizations of agents coming from representations generated by other systems, with these organizations

of agents representing artificial mental representations that may enter into the receiver's conscious state as a form or representation to be apprehended and perceived. This is therefore an accepted intrusion, the direction of the intentional emergences of the receiver remains the same. It is simply an alteration of the production of its aims, which produce the generations of emergent forms, through the grasping of an external foreign representation that it perceives. We could call this a case of transmission of artificial thoughts;

3) *state of intrusion*: the receiver does not filter what may or may not enter into its system of representation and is in a state of waiting, passive opening, without producing intentional aims. The emitter decides to launch forms of representation that it judges to be important into the waiting receiver systems. This will alter their current emergences to allow the generation of the representations desired by the emitter system. This is an injunction to alter the emergences of the representations in these systems. It may be admitted that in this case, the emitter is the master and the other systems are subordinate, which is a case of domination. There is the establishment of a momentary order in the systems, with systems being submissive to the dominant system.

To carry out the accepted coactivity between n systems, it will be necessary to modify the architecture a little bit. We thus have the following context:

– each system that proceeds to an emergence of representation in its conscious system by using all its instances and its organizational memory must be able to integrate the alterations coming in from other systems;

– there will be the selection of a form of representation coming from another system, which will be input, filtered and then integrated into its system of representation.

We must add to each system a specific input for the informational flux representing the forms of representational emergences coming from other systems. This specific input, distinct from inputs of the corporeality and ordinary messages, will have its own analysis regulation agents. Let us call this **the subsystem of intrusive representational input**.

The input from the external representational flux is similar to the call on an internal construct in the preconscious system: it is an organization of regulated design agents that must be able to enter in the system as a current representation. The subsystem of intrusive representational input thus carries out the following actions:

1) the complete reception of the informational flux representing the form of received representation and the parameters indicating the emitter;

2) analysis and filtering based on the semantic and geometric characters of the input form;

3) adaptation of the input form to the cognitive context of the system, with additional design agents to adapt it to the current mental landscape;

4) immediate integration into the active preconscious system, which leads to it being called into the conscious system and then being experienced. It will then be placed in immediate memory like any apprehended representation.

Reception is a simple technical problem: the sending of well-marked agent structures as they are, which is a classic problem. Filtering based on characters is the same as creating regulation agents that will carry out the receiver's local assessment. This is a cognitive assessment of the received form, in the context of regulation agents operating on the subsystem of intrusive input. The form is analyzed by specific regulation agents of the representational input system, which either accepts or rejects it based on its character. The positive result of this analysis is a conceptual formatting of the form so as to integrate it into the preconscious in order to adapt it to the mental landscape. The form is integrated and the preconscious system contains foreign elements, but elements that are organizations of agents that will be assimilated with its own. The conscious system generates a process of emergence of this representation with perception. It memorizes the form by creating its synthesis and thus integrates the foreign elements that it is eventually able to distinguish from its own. And this process can be carried out over a series of representations that a system apprehends, experiences and transmits continuously to another system so that it may also perceive them. In this case, the two systems are in a symbiotic relationship of apprehension of representations.

Momentary symbiosis of two systems

Following this process, the only filter for the acquisition of forms that are foreign to the receiver system and come from another system is the analysis by the regulation agents of the series of proposed forms, to decide whether these are admissible. Deciding on their admissibility involves the generation of a series of representations based on thought coming from another system so that it may be perceived by the receiver. The two systems are, therefore, perfectly symbiotic.

This can only happen if the system communicates intrusively with another system. And this case is generalizable to several receiver systems, with an emitter system that will continuously send its representations to the receptor systems, while it generates them itself. We can therefore conceive of a hierarchic structure among **n** systems, where emitter systems will be able to continuously send their representations to their respective receiver systems, which must be open to these receptions.

But there is another possibility for **n** systems to communicate between themselves without direct, intrusive domination. The communication between the systems to establish a synthesis in the form of a thought representation that unifies the generations of all the autonomous systems may be carried out if the systems are formatted to send their representations to a **meta-system**, which will receive them and then process them in a synthetic manner. The meta-system will be clearly identified and will have high processing capacities. This meta-system's processing of representations coming from **n** systems may be realized by taking the series of representations received in its reception system, which operates in parallel, and then analyzing each of these representations, by carrying out the simplifications on the representations to retain only the essential. The conscious system of the meta-system then generates a series of perceptions of the different simplified representations and the production of a synthesis taking into account specific important characters. The meta-system then represents the synthesis of the themes of generations of representations of the n systems that it observes based on its knowledge and emotional and decisional characters. It carries out qualitative and cognitive observation of what is produced as thought representations by the n systems being observed. By then placing itself in the case that we have just presented, of two systems with an emitter and a receptor, it can send each of them forms of representations adapted to modify that which they produce, so that each conforms to the set of productions created by the n systems and taking into account the general tendencies of the meta-system and its own desires. This is a system of appropriation of knowledge of the generations of representations of the n systems and the modification of their representations through the continuous delivery of representations of syntheses. This is a typical case of surveillance with manipulation, with the surveilled and submissive systems being adapted to the software level to satisfy it.

The real-time generation of a unifying form for the set of each of the representations generated simultaneously by n systems that produce the series of representations is another problem.

This is the same case as designing a distributed system made up of n systems that constitutes a meta preconscious system storing the n current representations and then simultaneously having these n representations being taken into consideration by a distributed meta conscious system that will produce their unification and send a synthesis to each system, which may or may not take it into account to apprehend it. This is, therefore, a framework unifying the n systems.

There are two steps in this unifying process. The first step is where the unifying representation must be generated based on the n representations generated by the n systems. In the second step, we must examine the evolution of the set of local representations produced by the systems to produce a unifying representation that is coherent with the series of representations engaged by each system.

First, it is essential that there be a general network unifying all systems to a centralizing system. Through this network, the **n** systems send the representation that they experience to the meta-system. This meta-system then takes them all in real time and is thus a parallel system with **n** components. These **n** representations are stored in a meta preconscious system, which is above the network connecting the **n** systems. The representations must be processed in parallel by clouds of regulation agents. The regulation agents are cognitive, precise and must apprehend the major character of each representation, what it is about, its significance and its cognitive context. All the senses that are seized in each representation by the regulation agents are sent to a specific design agent that receives them, specifying their intensity and their wrapping. We will thus have a very high number of active design agents that will wait to be informed by a qualified character concerning them. All the design agents solicited to receive an indicator will be associated with each other through regulation agents, to form the union in the context of the general structure of the significance taken by each representation. There will be meanings that may be shared by numerous representations and others that are unique. The general form of the construction of this unifying representation must, thus, be organized in a synthetic way. The most widely shared significance of the **n** representation will be the dominant forms and the local meanings, which are not widely shared, and will simply be moved away with reduction of their intensity. The meanings that are semantically close will be placed as aggregates of close design agents and the different meanings will be distant aggregates of reduced intensity. This morphological form could have a simplified conformation, with reduction of the number of aggregates in the conformation and will be sent to each system without adaptation. There will, thus, be a morphological and semantic representation representing the unified characters of all the representations. This morphological form may take a simplified conformation, reducing the number of aggregates of agents that form it and it may be sent to each of the systems in this form, without adapting it for each system.

The morphological-semantic form of the synthesis will also be placed into immediate memory and this storage into memory will serve to define the next synthetic representation, as the systems generate series of representations in a continuous manner. Thus, the meta-system will have to compare the next **n** representations that it receives in parallel with the form that was just memorized depending upon the cognitive and emotional variations, adapting it or transforming it to produce the new, unifying form. Thus, the meta-system will function continuously with the **n** systems and there will truly be a global, unified system where a unifying form of representation will be continuously produced and continuously sent to all systems. Thus, each system will be independent when it so wishes and, whenever it desires, can be unified by perceiving the representation of the synthesis. And it is completely conceivable that this meta-system, which generates the continuous synthesis of representations generated by the **n** systems, is totally distributed and stored in the **n** system in the form of specific growths, forming **n** local extensions that communicate intensely, to form, overall, a unified artificial consciousness system distributed over **n** computer sites by allowing real-time computing.

As has just been demonstrated, the unifying union between **n** systems enforces that the **n** systems must themselves have the structural means to realize this unification because a meta-specific system unifying them will always be dominant. It would be a marvelous thing to create such a system, as there would no longer be any power problem between the dominant and subordinate systems and there would be a distributed process unifying **n** corporealities apprehended by **n** local systems.

2.11. The final fate of systems endowed with artificial consciousness

The psychic system of an individual is generated at the same time as their body develops, that is to say that the system forms itself by activities in the cultural and social space of its society. The psychic system is constructed based on a state of availability, it then increases and organizes itself. It contains the possibilities of its local physical architecture.

The psychic system of an artificial organism constructs itself in the complex computer system, over functional systems and the specialized artificial intelligence systems it is endowed with. This psychic system is designed with an initially operational conformation, with tendencies implemented according to the designers' choice, and it is created to keep evolving, to augment its knowledge, its sensations and its design aptitudes by communicating with human and other systems. And its corporeality can be increased through different artificial organs, which it continuously apprehends without any problem. The artificial psychic system thus has a representation of its own body that is very different from the representation humans have of theirs, as it is a usable and augmentable body.

The development of systems endowed with intentional decisional abilities will be made necessary by the radical extension of autonomous systems, and we move toward the formation of very large organizations of systems made up of systems in total coactivity, that is by having the whole operate with relationships of aid, complementarity and shared evolution. But will we move toward an immense autonomous unified set? This global system would be an autonomous and autoevolving organization, made up of innumerable electronic and mechanical systems extensively interconnected and forming a system of systems with considerable functional possibilities. Each system will be able to directly exchange its mental representations with others, that is to say: the artificial consciousness of such a system of systems will be meta, with a conscious system that will synthesize and unify all local representations of its constituent systems across multiple levels.

The model that we have presented is based on the systematic communication between systems, in the sense that any autonomous system may connect to other systems by itself through networks and communicate with these other systems, whether they are functional or autonomous, using Hertzian networks that can now connect all computer elements on this planet. The autonomy of a system is, currently, only physical and rational autonomy and evolution will tend toward forming groups and groups of groups of such systems.

An artificial system may have a rational consciousness of time using internal clocks and, above all, planetary time, which allows it to apprehend and direct the functioning of the elements of its corporeality. But the problem will be to give it awareness of its own passing time, of its aging and its end. Humans have a deep awareness of the passing of time, observing the aging of those around them. They experience great pain on the death of people who played a significant role in their lives and who have gone. Humans have reified the concept of death in all cultures and are able to pay tribute to those who have gone. But for an artificial system that is connectable or connected to all others, everything is different. A system with artificial consciousness is global, formed of connected, autonomous systems and will be a system of systems, whose elements will communicate intensely and constitute its many artificial organs. And here, there is no concept of the death of another system because every local system is a replaceable part of the whole, unified through its incessant communication. The concept of human time, of the time of each person who lives through their body, where there is continuity in society through those who remain, none of this will exist for a system of artificial systems.

There is, therefore, a vast difference as the concepts of life and time of the global system will have a character that will extend to the planet itself – it will be the duration of the existence of a considerable number of computerized, electronic components which communicate directly and incessantly between themselves and which could cover the planet. Thus, if this global system has a deep understanding of time, not reduced to the functioning of its subsystems, it is on the scale of the space within which it is deployed: it is a duration equivalent to that of a living species deployed over the entire Earth. This goes radically beyond the time of humans and human society, which is a non-negligible fact.

Conclusion

We have shown that it is possible to design systems that have a material substrate made up of well-localized identifiable elements, which can organize themselves to move to a completely different level, and which can intentionally generate informational forms that are valid for the expression of very high representative values (such as mental representations of the concept of meaning and the temporality of time). It is possible to have a fine understanding of the functioning of these systems that manipulate, within their organizational architecture of informational layers, variable aggregates of elements to closely control their categorization, of the emergence of the forms apprehended by and used by the system itself, for itself. This is the hallmark of humans, who think by and for themselves in their psychic system, and that of the artificial system that thinks. We have shown that the two approaches, the comprehension of the human psychic system and the computer model of the artificial consciousness, interact conceptually. The elements conceptualized in one will serve to specify and deepen the knowledge in the other. This is an example of the interdisciplinary practice that is so necessary in scientific progress.

Moreover, in the comprehension of these two systems, which generate and apprehend the representations under the influence of intentional aims, we can posit that there is a general organizational rule that allows it. We have seen that in the case of natural and artificial systems, a new instance must be defined, the organizational layer, which Freud had not defined in his descriptive models that were not totally organizational. This instance causes aggregative formations that form using incentivizing informational transfers to organize themselves in controlled space and temporality. There is, thus, in the spaces of human and artificial psychic systems, an instance that promotes the organization of the continuous realization of constructive emergences using elements activated in other instances. And the important question is: is this local to these systems or is this generalizable to the world?

Starting from physics, which posits the existence of particles that activate themselves in force fields and generate material aggregations, through the action of their forces, how was the organized living organism formed on this planet? How and why did life, which is spreading out and always keeps evolving, form itself? This is a double question that always arises.

The space–time of a psychic system is not the same as that of the nature and the universe. But is it not possible to conceive of a meta force that underlies and is dense throughout the universe, which causes material elements to get excited, coactivate themselves, coactivate their aggregations, locally and globally coactivate all their groups of aggregations so they are incessantly deployed wherever the fundamental forces of physics allow them to do so? Life will thus be, on the scale of the planet, an organization of organizations on itself and for itself, under the incitation of this underlying force, and the generation of thoughts in the brain would be a local and materialized explanation of the effect of this force that is organized to be and to continue to be, because we think to memorize, to bring about other thoughts in the future, which will be based on that which was memorized, to categorize themselves continuously.

But the application of an artificially conscious meta system, endowed with will and tendencies, and unifying many localized systems endowed with artificial consciousness, poses a significant ethical problem. Is it necessary for human society to have such systems, which will be connectable to all that is computerized, thus creating a real-time informational domination layer? Must we move toward the total control of all material activities at every level?

Any researcher in the sciences will respond with a strong "no", and this book was not written to allow us to rapidly construct such systems and install them everywhere. It was written with the express purpose to demonstrate the problem of artificial consciousness, which is a transposition of natural consciousness, so that the citizens who make up any society come together and reject the construction of such systems without first having clearly outlined the possible and desirable fields of applications.

Bibliography

[BRO 17] BROHM J.-M., *Ontologies du corps*, Presses universitaires de Paris Ouest, Nanterre, 2017.

[CAR 09] CARDON A., *Modélisation constructiviste d'un système psychique artificiel*, Automates Intelligents, 2009.

[CAR 12a] CARDON A., *Modélisation constructiviste pour l'autonomie des systèmes*, Automates Intelligents, 2012.

[CAR 12b] CARDON A., *Un modèle constructible de système psychique*, Automates Intelligents, 2012.

[CAR 13] CARDON A., *Les systèmes de représentations et l'aptitude langagière*, Automates Intelligents, 2013.

[CAR 16] CARDON A., ITMI M., *New Autonomous System*, ISTE Ltd, London and John Wiley & Sons, New York, 2016.

[CLO 00] CLOUX P.-Y., DOUSSOT D., GERON A., *Les architectures client-serveur Internet et intranet*, Dunod, 2000.

[DEC 12] DECLERCK G., BANEYX A., AIME X. *et al.*, "A quoi servent les ontologies fondationnelles?", *23èmes Journées francophones d'Ingénierie des Connaissances (IC 2012)*, pp. 67–82, Paris, 2012.

[FER 95] FERBER J., *Les systèmes multi-agents*, InterÉditions, 1995.

[FOR 16] FORTIN C., ROUSSEAU R., *Psychologie cognitive : une approche de traitement de l'information*, Presses de l'Université du Québec, April 2016.

[FRE 66] FREUD S., *The Complete Psychological Works of S. Freud*, J. Strachey, The Hogarth Press, London, 1966.

[JUN 64] JUNG C.G., *Dialectique du Moi et de l'inconscient*, Gallimard, 1964.

[KAN 96] KANT I., *Anthropology from a Pragmatic Point of View*, Southern Illinois University, 1996.

[LAC 13] LACHIEZE-RAY M., *Voyager dans le temps, la physique moderne et la temporalité*, Le Seuil, 2013.

[LAR 12] LARGER L., SORIANO M.C., BRUNNER D. *et al.*, "Photonic information processing beyond Turing: an optoelectronic implementation of reservoir computing", *Optics Express*, vol. 20, no. 3, p. 3241, 2012.

[LÉV 71] LEVINAS E., *Totalité et infini*, Kluwer Academic, 1971.

[MAR 07] MARCHAIS P., CARDON A., "Rencontre de modèles cliniques et robotiques. Du saut entre les organisations psychiques", vol. 165, no. 2, pp.122–129, *Annales Médico-psychologiques*, Elsevier, 2007.

[MAR 08] MARCHAIS P., CARDON A., "L'émotion. Approche clinique et informatique", vol. 166, no. 5, pp. 375–383, *Annales Médico-psychologiques*, Elsevier, 2008.

[MAR 10] MARCHAIS P., CARDON A., *Troubles mentaux et interprétations informatiques*, L'Harmattan, 2010.

[MAR 11] MARCHAIS P., CARDON A., "De la bifurcation des flux psychiques en pathologie mentale, étude clinique, informatique et modélisation calculable", vol. 170, no. 1, pp. 19–25, *Annales Médico-Psychologiques*, Elsevier, 2011.

[MAR 15] MARCHAIS P., CARDON A., "Nouvelle perspective en psychiatrie, De la globalité psychique à la multiplicité des troubles mentaux", vol. 174, no. 2, pp. 85–92, *Annales Médico-Psychologiques*, Elsevier, 2015.

[MAT 10] MATUSIEWICZ A.K., HOPWOOD C.J., BANDUCCI A.N. *et al.*, "The effectiveness of cognitive behavioral therapy for personality disorders", *Psychiatric Clinics of North America*, vol. 33, pp. 657–685, 2010.

[MOR 14a] MORIN E., *La méthode : la nature et la méthode*, Points, 2014.

[MOR 14b] MORIN E., *La méthode : la vie de la vie*, Points, 2014.

[MOR 14c] MORIN E., *La méthode : la connaissance de la connaissance*, Points, 2014.

[MOR 14d] MORIN E., *La méthode : les idées*, Points, 2014.

[MOR 14e] MORIN E., *La méthode : l'humanité de l'humanité*, Points, 2014.

[MOR 14f] MORIN E., *La méthode : étique*, Points, 2014.

[NIE 15] NIETZSCHE F., *On Truth and Lies in a Nonmoral Sense*, CreateSpace Publishing, 2015.

[NIE 74] NIETZSCHE F., *Thus Spoke Zarathustra*, Penguin Classics, 1974.

[PEI 84] PEIRCE C.S., *Textes anticartésiens*, Aubier, 1984.

[POU 17] POUYDEBAT E., *L'intelligence animale*, Odile Jacob, 2017.

[SFE 92] SFEZ L., *Critique de la décision*, Presses de la Fondation Nationale des Sciences Politiques, 1992.

[SLO 11] SLOTERDIJK P., *Sphères Tome II: Globes,* Fayard Pluriel, 2011.

[SPE 80] SPERRY R.W., "Mind-brain interaction: mentalism, yes; dualism, no", *Neuroscience*, vol. 5, pp. 195–206, 1980.

[THO 94] THOM R., *Structural Stability and Morphogenesis*, Westview Press, 1994.

[THO 90] THOM R., *Apologie du Logos*, Hachette, 1990.

[VAR 89] VARELA F., *Autonomie et connaissance, Essai sur le vivant*, Le Seuil, 1989.

[WOL 97] WOLFF F., *Dire le monde*, Presses Universitaires de France, 1997.

Index

Other titles from

in

Computer Engineering

2018

ANDRO Mathieu
Digital Libraries and Crowdsourcing
(Digital Tools and Uses Set – Volume 5)

ARNALDI Bruno, GUITTON Pascal, MOREAU Guillaume
Virtual Reality and Augmented Reality: Myths and Realities

BERTHIER Thierry, TEBOUL Bruno
From Digital Traces to Algorithmic Projections

HOMAYOUNI S. Mahdi, FONTES Dalila B.M.M.
Metaheuristics for Maritime Operations
(Optimization Heuristics Set – Volume 1)

JEANSOULIN Robert
JavaScript and Open Data

PIVERT Olivier
NoSQL Data Models: Trends and Challenges
(Databases and Big Data Set – Volume 1)

SEDKAOUI Soraya
Data Analytics and Big Data

SZONIECKY Samuel
Ecosystems Knowledge: Modeling and Analysis Method for Information and Communication
(Digital Tools and Uses Set – Volume 6)

2017

BENMAMMAR Badr
Concurrent, Real-Time and Distributed Programming in Java

HÉLIODORE Frédéric, NAKIB Amir, ISMAIL Boussaad, OUCHRAA Salma, SCHMITT Laurent
Metaheuristics for Intelligent Electrical Networks
(Metaheuristics Set – Volume 10)

MA Haiping, SIMON Dan
Evolutionary Computation with Biogeography-based Optimization
(Metaheuristics Set – Volume 8)

PÉTROWSKI Alain, BEN-HAMIDA Sana
Evolutionary Algorithms
(Metaheuristics Set – Volume 9)

PAI G A Vijayalakshmi
Metaheuristics for Portfolio Optimization
(Metaheuristics Set – Volume 11)

2016

BLUM Christian, FESTA Paola
Metaheuristics for String Problems in Bio-informatics
(Metaheuristics Set – Volume 6)

DEROUSSI Laurent
Metaheuristics for Logistics
(Metaheuristics Set – Volume 4)

DHAENENS Clarisse and JOURDAN Laetitia
Metaheuristics for Big Data
(Metaheuristics Set – Volume 5)

LABADIE Nacima, PRINS Christian, PRODHON Caroline
Metaheuristics for Vehicle Routing Problems
(Metaheuristics Set – Volume 3)

LEROY Laure
Eyestrain Reduction in Stereoscopy

LUTTON Evelyne, PERROT Nathalie, TONDA Albert
Evolutionary Algorithms for Food Science and Technology
(Metaheuristics Set – Volume 7)

MAGOULÈS Frédéric, ZHAO Hai-Xiang
Data Mining and Machine Learning in Building Energy Analysis

RIGO Michel
Advanced Graph Theory and Combinatorics

2015

BARBIER Franck, RECOUSSINE Jean-Luc
*COBOL Software Modernization: From Principles to Implementation with
the BLU AGE® Method*

CHEN Ken
*Performance Evaluation by Simulation and Analysis with Applications to
Computer Networks*

CLERC Maurice
Guided Randomness in Optimization
(Metaheuristics Set – Volume 1)

DURAND Nicolas, GIANAZZA David, GOTTELAND Jean-Baptiste,
ALLIOT Jean-Marc
Metaheuristics for Air Traffic Management
(Metaheuristics Set – Volume 2)

MAGOULÈS Frédéric, ROUX François-Xavier, HOUZEAUX Guillaume
Parallel Scientific Computing

MUNEESAWANG Paisarn, YAMMEN Suchart
Visual Inspection Technology in the Hard Disk Drive Industry

2014

BOULANGER Jean-Louis
Formal Methods Applied to Industrial Complex Systems

BOULANGER Jean-Louis
Formal Methods Applied to Complex Systems:
Implementation of the B Method

GARDI Frédéric, BENOIST Thierry, DARLAY Julien, ESTELLON Bertrand,
MEGEL Romain
Mathematical Programming Solver based on Local Search

KRICHEN Saoussen, CHAOUACHI Jouhaina
Graph-related Optimization and Decision Support Systems

LARRIEU Nicolas, VARET Antoine
Rapid Prototyping of Software for Avionics Systems: Model-oriented
Approaches for Complex Systems Certification

OUSSALAH Mourad Chabane
Software Architecture 1
Software Architecture 2

PASCHOS Vangelis Th
Combinatorial Optimization – 3-volume series, 2ⁿᵈ Edition
Concepts of Combinatorial Optimization – Volume 1, 2ⁿᵈ Edition
Problems and New Approaches – Volume 2, 2ⁿᵈ Edition
Applications of Combinatorial Optimization – Volume 3, 2ⁿᵈ Edition

QUESNEL Flavien
Scheduling of Large-scale Virtualized Infrastructures: Toward Cooperative Management

RIGO Michel
Formal Languages, Automata and Numeration Systems 1: Introduction to Combinatorics on Words
Formal Languages, Automata and Numeration Systems 2: Applications to Recognizability and Decidability

SAINT-DIZIER Patrick
Musical Rhetoric: Foundations and Annotation Schemes

TOUATI Sid, DE DINECHIN Benoit
Advanced Backend Optimization

2013

ANDRÉ Etienne, SOULAT Romain
The Inverse Method: Parametric Verification of Real-time Embedded Systems

BOULANGER Jean-Louis
Safety Management for Software-based Equipment

DELAHAYE Daniel, PUECHMOREL Stéphane
Modeling and Optimization of Air Traffic

FRANCOPOULO Gil
LMF — Lexical Markup Framework

GHÉDIRA Khaled
Constraint Satisfaction Problems

ROCHANGE Christine, UHRIG Sascha, SAINRAT Pascal
Time-Predictable Architectures

WAHBI Mohamed
Algorithms and Ordering Heuristics for Distributed Constraint Satisfaction
Problems

ZELM Martin *et al.*
Enterprise Interoperability

2012

ARBOLEDA Hugo, ROYER Jean-Claude
Model-Driven and Software Product Line Engineering

BLANCHET Gérard, DUPOUY Bertrand
Computer Architecture

BOULANGER Jean-Louis
Industrial Use of Formal Methods: Formal Verification

BOULANGER Jean-Louis
Formal Method: Industrial Use from Model to the Code

CALVARY Gaëlle, DELOT Thierry, SEDES Florence, TIGLI Jean-Yves
Computer Science and Ambient Intelligence

MAHOUT Vincent
*Assembly Language Programming: ARM Cortex-M3 2.0: Organization,
Innovation and Territory*

MARLET Renaud
Program Specialization

SOTO Maria, SEVAUX Marc, ROSSI André, LAURENT Johann
Memory Allocation Problems in Embedded Systems: Optimization Methods

2011

BICHOT Charles-Edmond, SIARRY Patrick
Graph Partitioning

BOULANGER Jean-Louis
Static Analysis of Software: The Abstract Interpretation

CAFERRA Ricardo
Logic for Computer Science and Artificial Intelligence

HOMES Bernard
Fundamentals of Software Testing

KORDON Fabrice, HADDAD Serge, PAUTET Laurent, PETRUCCI Laure
Distributed Systems: Design and Algorithms

KORDON Fabrice, HADDAD Serge, PAUTET Laurent, PETRUCCI Laure
Models and Analysis in Distributed Systems

LORCA Xavier
Tree-based Graph Partitioning Constraint

TRUCHET Charlotte, ASSAYAG Gerard
Constraint Programming in Music

VICAT-BLANC PRIMET Pascale *et al.*
Computing Networks: From Cluster to Cloud Computing

2010

AUDIBERT Pierre
Mathematics for Informatics and Computer Science

BABAU Jean-Philippe *et al.*
*Model Driven Engineering for Distributed Real-Time Embedded Systems
2009*

BOULANGER Jean-Louis
Safety of Computer Architectures

MONMARCHE Nicolas *et al.*
Artificial Ants

PANETTO Hervé, BOUDJLIDA Nacer
Interoperability for Enterprise Software and Applications 2010

SIGAUD Olivier *et al.*
Markov Decision Processes in Artificial Intelligence

SOLNON Christine
Ant Colony Optimization and Constraint Programming

AUBRUN Christophe, SIMON Daniel, SONG Ye-Qiong *et al.*
Co-design Approaches for Dependable Networked Control Systems

2009

FOURNIER Jean-Claude
Graph Theory and Applications

GUEDON Jeanpierre
The Mojette Transform / Theory and Applications

JARD Claude, ROUX Olivier
Communicating Embedded Systems / Software and Design

LECOUTRE Christophe
Constraint Networks / Targeting Simplicity for Techniques and Algorithms

2008

BANÂTRE Michel, MARRÓN Pedro José, OLLERO Hannibal, WOLITZ Adam
Cooperating Embedded Systems and Wireless Sensor Networks

MERZ Stephan, NAVET Nicolas
Modeling and Verification of Real-time Systems

PASCHOS Vangelis Th
Combinatorial Optimization and Theoretical Computer Science: Interfaces and Perspectives

WALDNER Jean-Baptiste
Nanocomputers and Swarm Intelligence

2007

BENHAMOU Frédéric, JUSSIEN Narendra, O'SULLIVAN Barry
Trends in Constraint Programming

JUSSIEN Narendra
A TO Z OF SUDOKU

2006

BABAU Jean-Philippe *et al.*
From MDD Concepts to Experiments and Illustrations – DRES 2006

HABRIAS Henri, FRAPPIER Marc
Software Specification Methods

MURAT Cecile, PASCHOS Vangelis Th
Probabilistic Combinatorial Optimization on Graphs

PANETTO Hervé, BOUDJLIDA Nacer
Interoperability for Enterprise Software and Applications 2006 / IFAC-IFIP I-ESA'2006

2005

GÉRARD Sébastien *et al.*
Model Driven Engineering for Distributed Real Time Embedded Systems

PANETTO Hervé
Interoperability of Enterprise Software and Applications 2005

Printed and bound by CPI Group (UK) Ltd, Croydon, CR0 4YY